CRAFTING
THE SALE

CRAFTING
THE SALE

Drive Revenue, Impress Buyers, and Transform Your Career

MICHAEL TUSO

GIRL FRIDAY BOOKS

GFB GIRL FRIDAY BOOKS

Published by Girl Friday Books™, Seattle
www.girlfridaybooks.com
Produced by Girl Friday Productions

Cover: Megan Katsanevakis
Development & editorial: Dan Crissman
Production editorial: Jaye Whitney Debber
Project management: Reshma Kooner

ISBN (paperback): 978-1-954854-02-4
ISBN (ebook): 978-1-954854-07-9

Library of Congress Control Number: 2023906439
First edition

To my mom, Florence

CONTENTS

THE HARD SELLER

WHY OLD-SCHOOL SALES TECHNIQUES DON'T WORK ANYMORE

I really did not want to lie down on this bed.

Please don't make me, I thought to myself. *Oh god, here she goes. She's going to make me do it.*

The next thing I knew, I was lying on an $8,000 mattress I had no intention of buying.

The salesperson had practically been salivating when she greeted my partner and me at the door. I read the expression on her face, and the slight upward curl at the corners of her lips told me everything I needed to know. We fit the "affluent millennial" profile she had been waiting for all day.

"What can I help you find?"

"We need a new bed," I said tentatively.

"You've come to the right place," she said without missing a beat. "Do you know what Restoration Hardware is as a style?"

I took a big yet unassuming sigh. "Yes."

"Oh gosh, I just knew you two would."

"Because we're a gay couple?" I whispered to my partner. I couldn't help myself with the inference.

Her pupils dilated some more as I felt her trying to jump into my wallet headfirst.

"I think I have the perfect one. Right this way."

In an unfortunate series of events that redirected us from what we came into the store for, suddenly I found myself lying on the most expensive bed in the showroom. I can see her logic now. If you can just get the customer to visualize what it will be like to have this bed—this majestic piece of gold disguised as memory foam—then they will have to buy it.

This woman is going to get me if I don't stop her, I thought. I work in sales; why was I letting her do this?

When my eyes opened back up, she was hovering over us like a cat toying with its meal.

"How do you like it?" As if anything but an affirmative would work.

Begrudgingly, I matched her enthusiasm. "Feels great."

She smiled approvingly, clearly pleased with how things were going. Then something caught her eye across the showroom. "Hold on one second—I have another customer that had a question. Don't you two go anywhere. I'll be right back."

As soon as she was out of sight, we ran for the doors and never looked back.

BUYING SHOULDN'T BE PAINFUL

What happens in your brain when someone tries to sell you something? Do you get excited? Do you feel annoyed? Do you put up a wall? Do you walk away? Do you feel nervous? Happy? Uncomfortable? Do conversations around money make you feel awkward? If so, why?

Now flip the scenario. What if you are the one selling?

How do you feel? Is the inclination to impress your viewpoint on others? Do you have a knee-jerk impulse to want to tell, explain, and pitch? *What is that knee-jerk experience* we see so often in ourselves and in other people?

Often, the impulse is exactly this: To pitch. To tell. To persuade. But deep down inside, a part of you feels that this approach is not quite right.

If you're like me, maybe you initially thought selling was describing. Before I got into sales, I thought the profession was solely about description: "Our service is better than our competitors'." "You won't find anyone who can beat our price." "This steak is dry aged for sixty days." But describing without knowing the audience feels a little bit like winging it. When you stop to think about it, does that ever work? Maybe, but shouldn't we know a little bit about them so we can have some inclination of how our pitch will land?

It's not just the pitch anymore, though. It's the emails that don't really help us solve problems or that simply promote product features instead. It's the calls that feel invasive instead of helping us solve problems. Our craft has been reduced to a single-minded fixation on "the sale" at all costs. In the meantime, we have lost our sense of the finer details. We have lost what it means to sell well. We fixate on the end itself without a clear blueprint of the "how" part of getting there. We could all benefit from slowing things down to help both ourselves and our prospects see a clearer picture.

Sellers today often come into the conversation with buyers at a much later point than they did previously. We also, on average, have less face time with buyers than ever before. The consulting firm Gartner projects that by 2025, nearly 80 percent of all client interactions will be conducted digitally. And today's buyers are also better informed. Before the internet, the seller often had the most up-to-date information on pricing, features, and the general lay of the land in specific markets. Today, buyers can go on Kelley Blue Book and find out what a car is worth. They can compare software products on G2. They can jump into a Slack group and get information directly from their most trusted source of information—other buyers. Since buyers are better informed, they now expect a certain experience, on a cultural and emotional level.

Compounding this issue, it is also easier than ever to build a bespoke product. Whether your product is software, a book like this one, or something physical, it has never in human history been easier to create and customize. This dynamic gives buyers options, and options are power. More options can be more confusing too. Time spent qualifying and searching for a tool, then staking your reputation on the success of said tool, is taxing.

This is where the sales experience can make all the difference in a buyer's decision. Today's sellers don't need to list every reason why their product is better. And they definitely should not engage in high-pressure sales. Instead, sellers should help buyers get to yes on their own by focusing on the finer details of selling and providing an exceptional sales experience.

When you think of selling this way, it completely flips the dynamic. To sell more means to pitch, smooth talk, lecture, persuade, influence. Do you want these things done to you? No. No one wants their own individual autonomy of choice thwarted by anyone. Therefore, many people are triggered as soon as they engage with salespeople. Buyers know what you're doing. As soon as they hear awkward, sales-y one-liners, the veil is broken. You've immediately been detected and labeled: "Salesperson." "Cares about their commission." And then they move on to the next person who will help them.

This doesn't mean we never ask for their business. Quite the opposite. We *ask* instead of *pressure*.

To be fair, we always have harsh criticisms for salespeople

We need to hit the "update" button on how we sell. We must do so if we want to get better at our craft, make more money, and escape the hamster wheel of poor buying experiences.

when we're the buyers, or even the observers. And then we deliver these same awkward experiences when we are the ones selling. But focusing on being crafters of the sale, having a real human conversation without the awkwardness, takes practice and consciousness. We need to be direct, conversational, light, and fun. This lightness attracts buyers because it allows for us to deliver new information to them without taking away their need to solve problems on their own.

What about picking up on social cues—like when someone says something, we respond to them with the way they want to be treated? Tolerance for less-than-stellar experiences is diminishing rapidly. I fundamentally believe this is a good thing for the industry. Out with leading with the idea of persuading people for personal gain and in with solving real, acutely painful problems for our buyers.

We, the sellers, have a hugely important role in this paradigm shift. In today's world, we must take personal accountability for our own learning in sales and transform the way we are selling. We need to hit the "update" button on how we sell. We must do so if we want to get better at our craft, make more money, and escape the hamster wheel of poor buying experiences. Gone are the days of high-pressure selling. Gone are the days of business being about me, me, me. Sales is getting harder, yes, but buying is getting even harder. Recognizing and aligning to that can only help us.

The solutions to these problems are simple but not easy:

- First, as a seller, you must learn to resist the knee-jerk reaction to begin with yourself (or your product) and instead start with the buyer.
- Second, you must provide a different and better sales experience than your competitors.
- Third, you must be radically easy to understand and work with.

 Fourth and last, you must understand your buyer's view of the world.

WHY I WROTE THIS BOOK

I wrote this book because I saw over the course of my career that even the smallest improvements in how we sell can lead to monumental results. I would notice someone with raw talent that I just knew could do even better, and I saw the effects that even a modest amount of coaching would have not just on their short-term performance but also on their entire career.

I would see low performers move income brackets and figure out how to make sales a sustainable career. I would see top performers bring home paychecks that allowed them to travel the world, build families, and reach new heights that would have been out of reach for them in other careers. I would see people literally lift themselves out of poverty through the commitment of learning how to get better at sales.

This book was simply my chance to share with a broader audience my learnings from coaching on the front lines of sales teams. I don't expect you to agree with everything I say. I consider this book more of a guide to help you think about sales and a way to elevate your own craft. But at the end of the day, this book is about what has worked and not worked for me. Because sales is such a soft skill, with elements of art and science tossed together, it is impossible for anyone to claim total authority over a vast discipline that involves complex human psychology, money, corporate politics, prospecting, closing, forecasting, and so much more. We all have strengths and weaknesses, we are all students of the craft, and we all must learn from each other.

But I also wrote this book for another reason. I wrote this book because I rarely have good experiences when I am buying, and I saw that with just a little bit of training, sales-people can get vastly better at understanding what makes buyers tick. When they do this, they can significantly increase their commissions, deliver results for their companies, and be proud of their work. I have observed on the front lines a very different reality than what I have heard from many sales leaders. It wasn't that people lacked raw talent alone. It's that they lacked *know-how*. So, what if we showed them how? I've found when provided this know-how coupled with support, most sellers can radically improve their results.

I first noticed this dynamic while working for a Fortune 500 company. The leadership set sales targets and quotas, then simply crossed their fingers and hoped that the salespeople would figure it out for themselves. The sellers then experienced high levels of stress and burnout, which led to constant turn-over. The motto became "Hire faster, fire faster." The trauma of working in this environment made me understand the value of training and mentoring. I also wanted to know *why* people were or were not successful in sales.

I grew up where money was not readily available. I was raised by a single mom. My first job ever was as a karate in-structor; that's where I really honed my love for coaching peo-ple. Watching them improve was what made me tick. It still is what makes me tick. I was good at the art myself, but I came alive when I was helping others. Not just in the generic "I want to help people" way, but in the meaningful way where you see someone get significantly better because of working with you.

These early experiences shaped my beliefs around coach-ing and training. I learned that if you support people, truly support them, your company will do well too. I also learned that if you give a little more effort during onboarding, your people can ramp up faster. By training people and not just letting them learn on the fly, you can build a consistent and lasting team culture that keeps everything moving forward. It

By training people and not just letting them learn on the fly, you can build a consistent and lasting team culture that keeps everything moving forward.

may seem like a simple idea, but if you hire the right people, you must then give them a place where they can grow and develop. You'd be surprised how uncommon this is in practice.

I'm not one of those people that believes a company is a family (run for the hills if you hear a company referring to its people as "family"). But good salespeople form a team, or better yet a tribe. In a family, we give unconditional love. In a tribe, we give unconditional growth. When we take care of our salespeople and give them the support they need, they flourish. It's hardwired into us to need and respond positively to environments like this.

After years of working for companies on both extremes—those that fostered environments that enabled their employees to thrive, and those that did not—I began to learn key differences in each type of organization. When it was my turn to build a sales team from scratch, I had the ability to create and build from the ground up. This was how I formulated and ultimately fortified my strategies of crafting the sale and began teaching them to others.

The results were drastically different. Prior to writing this book, I worked at a startup called Chili Piper as its first sales leader. The team had just two sellers when I joined, and the company had not yet reached $1 million in recurring revenue. By the time I left in 2021, the organization had a more than nine-figure valuation, with dozens of sellers on its sales team. The focus in the early days of building the company was squarely on providing the best possible buying experience and on developing the skills of the sales team itself. By making it easy to buy at every stage of the process, we posited, we would be able to grow faster than our competition. And by having a sales team that was prepared to handle the complex job of selling, we became one of the fastest-growing startups anywhere. Though I've since moved on to cofound Callypso, the culture we built in those early days of Chili Piper's sales team remains top of mind. To me, that is what crafting the sale is all about.

HOW TO USE THIS BOOK

This book is about two things: how to create the best possible sales experiences that help us win more deals, and how to focus on the smaller details of selling. We will explore ways to make the selling process far less forced or adversarial. I believe that in doing so, not only do we create a better experience for our buyers, but we also end up being significantly more successful in driving revenue. In turn, we salespeople will be happier and build a more sustainable career where many have felt burnout.

Each chapter of this book will start with a story. Then we will move into the meat of the concepts of how to get better at crafting the sale as it relates to the chapter—these lessons will be in the subsections for each chapter. Each chapter will end with tactics and strategies—actionable pieces of information you can take with you to help you get better results.

Similar to how you might hit "update" on the software on your computer, this book is meant to enhance and uplift the way you sell. This book is also a cumulative exercise, serving as a guide that builds upon itself. So first we're going to set the stage by looking at things from the buyer's point of view and the sales experience. Then, in chapter 2, we will cover the timeless lessons surrounding confidence and desperation in sales, and how to use the latter to your advantage in the toughest situations.

In chapter 3, we will learn how critical discovery is in the sales motion, but in a way that speaks to a buyer's motivation. With this, we can start to learn what propels deals and what stagnates them.

Which leads us to chapter 4, where we will discuss the importance of habits, systems, and customization in sales. We will do the foundational work of replacing strategies that might have worked in the past but don't work today. We will also learn how to deploy the right tools at the right time.

In chapter 5, we will learn how to focus on efficiency and effectiveness in sales. We will take the opaque task of prospecting and break it down into digestible buckets we can get better at. In chapter 6, we will discover the power of reputation in sales and why personal brand matters more than ever—and when it doesn't.

The final two chapters are a distillation of the lessons I've learned over my decade-plus career in sales. In chapter 7, I will lay out the eight cardinal rules of selling that govern sales success. In chapter 8, I'll talk about how early in my career I had a panic attack and hit rock bottom, and why that experience counterintuitively taught me how to love sales.

Then, in our conclusion, we will answer the biggest question of all: Why do we even do all this in the first place? Because treating sales as a craft is better for the buyer; it's better for you, for me, for business, but most of all for *people*.

Let's jump in.

CHAPTER 1

HOW YOU SELL IS WHY THEY BUY

WHY THE SALES EXPERIENCE MATTERS MORE THAN EVER

Recently, I needed to purchase new HR and payroll software for my company, so I did my research on vendors and went to the website of my first choice, a well-established industry leader. After talking to an entry-level employee, I was scheduled with a more senior salesperson. This "senior" salesperson showed me a cookie-cutter slide-deck presentation about their company. It included their accolades, a company timeline, and publicly available information from the review website G2, which I had already referenced before our call. He then proceeded to tell me about all the other products his company offered that I did not want or need. The only real question he asked about my company was how much money I raised for the business.

My intention going into the call was to buy that day after getting a couple of questions answered. I had done my own research and only had a few technical questions about the product; I probably could have been closed in ten minutes start to finish. Instead, I ended up going with another vendor who didn't give me the hard sell. What should have been a no-brainer ten-minute close ended up being a lost opportunity.

So, what were the standard sales tactics that pushed me away? The biggest problem with the above scenario is that it was all take and no give. If there's one takeaway about sales that someone could ever glean, it's this: sales is about asking questions to solve problems—not telling, explaining, or pitching. Not asking questions for questions' sake but to uncover problems and help buyers solve them.

The salespeople I talked to did not try to understand why I wanted to buy their software. By asking *some* simple questions, they could have figured out that I had used the product before and came to them specifically because I liked what they offered. The one thing holding me back was a simple feature I wanted to learn more about. Instead of figuring out what I needed, both salespeople put me through a hyperstandardized process that did not apply to my specific situation.

OLD HABITS DIE HARD

The example above is unfortunately not an outlier; it is the norm. The buyer has a problem, then they do research and create a short list of vendors. Then they engage with their top choices. Usually at this point, the sellers start pressuring the buyer to choose them over their competitors.

So this prompts the question, Why do so many modern buying experiences feel so painful?

As it turns out, the modern *sales funnel* that most businesses use today is not so modern. It is credited to a man named

Elias St. Elmo Lewis, and he is said to have come up with the idea in 1898. You read that right. The "modern" funnel we use is more than a century old. The main parts of the sales funnel (also called *marketing funnel* and *AIDA model*) are attract attention, maintain interest, and create desire. There are slight variations of the model, but by and large the principle is the same: that sales is about getting our prospects to go through a series of linear steps, and that's how you create a customer. And while every company needs a well-defined sales process, I would argue that overly linear thinking alienates buyers and also dominates conventional thinking on sales floors.

The funnel is attractive to salespeople and sales leaders. The mind craves rationale. It craves the path of least resistance. I think this mental shortcut is why the funnel has persisted for so long. But in a post-internet world, we should consider looking at the model a little differently.

When buyers hop on calls with salespeople, their interactions often sound and feel outdated because the salespeople are still focused on themselves instead of the buyer. If we sellers are not careful, our process can place us as the buyer's savior instead of leaving room for the buyer to be the star. This generally happens when we sacrifice convenience for the sales experience. Think about the sellers I described above. They were the saviors. They had all the accolades in the conversation. But they also approached the sale that way because it was easier. It's easy to hop on calls and say the same thing every time and then hope some of them convert. It's much harder to think critically, be responsive to others' needs, and learn.

To fit nicely with this funnel, the sales profession invented a *structured sales call* for itself. It was popularized by several household-name tech companies, who were seen as the go-to for sales training of their time. The main idea behind a structured sales call is that you have very clearly delineated steps of a process that you want to run a buyer through. Yes, we all absolutely need a process to help us sell. However, I find what is most frequently lost is how we do the process.

The other problem with the structured sales call is that it comes across as one-sided and too rigid. Salespeople trained in an overly rigid sales process end up sounding canned and are more focused on process adherence than on tailoring their approach to the prospect and company they are working with. Combine this pressure to adhere to process with the pressure of quota attainment and a lack of coaching and training, and it becomes evident why so many salespeople struggle to build sustained careers in sales.

The sales funnel and the overly structured sales call are part of how we got here. Why we stay here is an entirely different story.

BREAKING THE MOLD

Salespeople today know that we can't boil the complicated task of trading our products for money down to a simple checklist of tasks. We know it's far more complex because we live it every day—it's more emotional than that. And also, by the time buyers talk to us, they are further along in their decision-making process, so the overall amount of time they spend with us has shrunk immensely. This means that when they do spend time with us, it needs to count.

I believe that the central problem of selling in today's world is that we haven't updated our strategies, tactics, and methodologies to reflect the changes that have impacted buying over the past few decades. We are still selling in what I like to call the *age of the seller*, where we held all the cards and information, and not the *age of the buyer*, where our prospects and customers have more control.

Our companies and products are *an* option, not the only option. What this means is that because buyers have more options than ever before, we should treat the buying process accordingly. Buyers don't have to work with us; they *choose* to work with us—this is why the sales experience is so critical and can make all the difference.

If you were to run through two product demos where the products were relatively similar and had all the features you wanted at the same price, what would be the very next thing you evaluated the companies on? The sales experience.

The sales experience becomes a microcosm of what it would be like to be a customer. Poor buying experiences come in many shapes and sizes. Did the seller listen and understand our needs, or did they give us a canned pitch? Did they seem knowledgeable about the product, or were they all over the place?

One of the most infamous sales practices in our space is the attempt to control our prospects and customers. You can see it in notable sales-training presentations and even famous books. The reality is that you can't ever really control another person. You can pressure, probe, and prod, but you can't ever control them. What would be better here is instead focusing on what we *can* control.

It amazes me when we pressure our buyers, because we know deep down that we don't respond to that type of selling ourselves. We think we are different from the people we are selling to; therein lies the gap. We are not different from our buyers.

The path forward is a clear one. We need to create space for the buyer. We need to abandon one-sided sales in favor of *conversational sales*. The best way to engage a buyer is to allow them to speak on their terms—rather than trying solely to control the outcome, instead helping them realize the outcome that is best for them. Oftentimes, talking less and allowing the customer to speak more helps our efforts to sell.

The reality is
no one cares
about what
you do until
you show them
what you can
do for them.

FRAMES OF REFERENCE

Being conversational in sales is the *give* approach to sales, where you invite the buyer to the conversation as an equal, where they are the hero of the story and you're there to help. It's a give-and-take, where the salesperson mostly uncovers problems through intentional discovery on an emotional level. And the best way to do that is to first try to understand where the buyer is coming from.

One of the chief complaints buyers have about salespeople is that they use their own frame of reference to try to project and influence their prospects instead of just being patient and really listening to what the prospects are saying—listening to understand instead of just listening for what they want to hear. Buyers can pick up on both ways.

People have infinitely different views and worldviews in business and their personal lives. Yet too often in the sales world, we treat people like factory lines, like each sale is exactly the same. Each sale is not the same. Each sale is wildly different because people's problems are different. I believe that seeing each call and sale differently helps us with active listening and being attuned to what other people are saying.

We should treat people the same when it comes to respect, professionalism, and dignity, but we should not when it comes to evaluating what tools to use in the context of helping the buyer solve a problem. This is because buyers can be at different points of their journey and bring with them different problems and perspectives. By recognizing that people are in different places, we take responsibility for helping them get where they need to go. The reality is no one cares about what you do until you show them what you can do for them.

We all have frames of reference that we operate from. Our job as salespeople is to understand where our buyer is coming from and where they want to go. Then we need to do the work to help them get there. Said differently, what is their view on any particular issue or topic of discussion?

Let's start with an easy example. Say you are a leasing agent at an apartment complex and a couple comes in and wants to inquire about the apartments you have available. They ask you what floor an available apartment is on. You reply, "It's on the second floor, but don't worry, the stairs are a quick walk and there's also an elevator."

But what if they wanted to be on the top floor because they are worried about noisy neighbors above them? This could be their attitude. Resisting our own internal desire to project onto a situation without knowing more about someone's motivations is paramount to sales success. It's more than not assuming, though. It's understanding their frame of reference: Where are they coming from? Why are we solving for something if we don't even know what they care about?

This dynamic happens all the time on all types of calls. The customer asks a question, and we immediately jump to solving for whatever the question was as if it were a problem to be solved. Often the best course of action here is to learn *more*, not to solve. We can start solving only when we understand the full picture.

In the scenario above, the best response would be something like this: "We have apartments available on the top floor, but also on the first floor. Did you all have a preference?" Going further in this instance means understanding why they are asking this question to begin with instead of assuming anything at all about their motives without knowing more. When a customer asks a question, it almost always means that there is something they care about behind that question. The important thing to note is not your answer or what you can do here. It's to know *why they asked this question to begin with.*

Tailoring our approach to our buyers is a must—especially through our line of questioning. Assuming is a habit we need to leave behind and replace with understanding. This can be done only through conscious awareness and practice. Through understanding, we can tailor to their worldview. Maybe they hate the feature you're discussing. Maybe they love it. As hard as it is to not project anything but love for your own product offering, what's more important is to elicit understanding of the frames of reference your buyers are operating under.

To take a different example, do you remember the debate about whether a dress was blue and black or white and gold that went viral on social media back in 2015? Some people saw an image of a dress that was blue and black. Others saw the dress as white and gold. Same dress, different colors. This is the ultimate illustration of how we can literally see different things when looking at the same exact photo. Don't be afraid to ask your buyers questions to see what they are seeing. Their reality might not match your own. That's why the first step is always to figure out where they are coming from.

One of the biggest areas of improvement when it comes to viewing reality clearly is the concept of *happy ears*—when you create a narrative in your head that something good will happen, usually that the customer will buy, simply because they use affirmative language or actions. The sad reality is many prospects don't want to hurt our feelings, so they say they love our products even though they have no intention of buying. Maybe they don't even have the power to buy. Our job as salespeople is to uncover, through thoughtful questioning and conversation, the *truth* and separate fiction from reality. Too often I've seen salespeople forecast deals that have no chance of closing because they heard what they wanted to hear from the buyer.

READ THE ROOM

Sometimes listening to understand is just the start, and what is most required is reading the room. At one point in my career, I sold to accountants. One day I was sent over a lead by another salesperson on my team. The lead was the owner of an accounting firm who was familiar with our product and very qualified. I could tell that he wanted to get right into it, and that he was already happy with the product based on previous experience. I just made sure he didn't have any questions or concerns, and then I went for it.

"Based on hearing you speak," I told him, "it sounds like you really need this tool and you know a lot about it already. I could be reading the room incorrectly, but would you want to go ahead and get started?" In just six minutes from the moment we started the call, he became a customer.

I don't tell this story to brag, but rather to illustrate the fact that I didn't exactly follow the advice of my manager or any of our trainings. We were encouraged to "follow the process" and basically ask a million questions and list all our accolades. Not doing that ended up being a win-win for everyone. I provided the optimal experience for the buyer and still got the desired result.

That said, there's a real difference in facilitating a sale, as with this example, and order taking. *Order taking* is when I go to Starbucks, they ask what type of coffee I want, and they give me what I ask for—it's transactional and involves no discovery other than product selection.

Facilitating comes in when you correctly read a prospect's intentions and deliver the right solution to meet the moment: you close the deal when they are ready, for example, and you don't jeopardize the short-term sale for the long-term implications of them being a customer. You understand that not all prospects will become customers today, and that's perfectly fine. You're trying to build trust so that when they are in market, you are who they go to. This comes with setting proper expectations and not exaggerating product features, and not burning leads by using pressure tactics or creating a poor sales experience.

This plays out in many types of sales roles. Many salespeople want all the leads to be like the accountant, who was ready to buy and required as little work as possible, but we know that is a very small percentage of deals. Most sales are not like the story above. They are full of friction and negotiation. Friction is not necessarily a bad thing. Friction in a sales cycle just means you must work to get the deal, not that you *can't* get the deal. Too often salespeople say deals are unwinnable because winning requires work to overcome buyers' fears or objections, to negotiate with them, to show them how your product will help them generate more revenue, and so on. Work to follow up and follow through. The earliest lesson I learned about sales was if you do the work that others in sales are unwilling to do, you will go infinitely further. This isn't about hustling or working harder. It's about working with intention.

MEET BUYERS WHERE THEY ARE

Part of working smarter is realizing that buyers come to us with all sorts of problems, levels of interest, expertise, information, and more. They come to us *differently*. Catering to this difference via the sales experience makes them feel appreciated, heard, and understood. So, task number one is figuring out where they are in their buyer's journey. Quite literally we need to *geographically locate* where they are—then we can help them get where they want and need to go.

Asking ourselves a few questions might help here:

- Where am I taking them?
- How am I giving instead of taking?
- Am I being conversational?
- How can I do better at picking up on social cues?
- How good of a job am I doing with follow-up and follow-through?
- How am I focusing on their journey instead of my own?
- Am I pitching, or am I helping them buy?

JOBS TO BE DONE

I am a big proponent of the Jobs to Be Done framework popularized by Anthony Ulwick. The simplified idea behind this term is that customers are "hiring" you and your product to do a "job" to help them accomplish their goals, progress in some way, or solve problems. Analyzing a sale through this lens is incredibly powerful in helping to navigate gaining traction and ultimately approval for your product.

This holds true in economically fruitful times as well as downturns. In downturns, I would even encourage people to think about what jobs can be "undone" by your product. For example, if "hiring" your software helps them save on headcount costs, that can be a massive area of motivation for companies.

Once we map out what jobs our product accomplishes, we need to understand a bit more about how we get hired for that job. Another way of referring to this dynamic is as the buyer's journey or process. Having a visual map or table here can help us go very far in better understanding how this can unfold. What does it take for the buyer to "hire" a vendor?

The following table shows my typical buying process for B2B technology.

THE B2B BUYER JOURNEY

STAGE OF BUYER JOURNEY	SALES ACTION
Buyer initially discovers a problem in their business.	Buyer may prioritize this against other problems and choose to act (or not).
Buyer commits to solving the problem.	Buyer ramps up research.
Buyer specifies the ideal solution to their problem.	Buyer makes note of all of their needs.
Buyer shifts from asking what they need to who can solve their problem best and fastest.	Buyer ramps up the search phase of finding the appropriate vendor.
Buyer identifies solutions and possible vendors.	Buyer narrows the decision down to a shortlist.
Buyer makes a decision.	Buyer agrees to sale or moves on.

The key with this table is to build awareness around where your buyer is currently and what steps need to be taken to get them where they need to go. Because many people treat prospects like they are all the same, without doing the task of geographically locating the buyer, the sales experience is always the same and they struggle to advance deals. They walk every buyer through the same exact regurgitated process without consideration of their needs. This is one reason why even modest enhancements to the sales experience go so far. The bar is low, and small improvements help you stand out from the competition in unimaginable ways. When they have short-listed you and you do provide a better experience, they will choose you. *How you sell is absolutely why they buy.*

With this graphic, we can start to slowly erode the gap between us and our buyers by understanding what it takes for them to get a deal done. The first thing that happens is a buyer becomes aware of a problem or improvement that can be made. Then they must decide to do something about it. After this they create their requirements and begin to scope out possible vendors (often referred to as the *RFP*, or *request for proposals*, stage). They then narrow down their choice of vendors, and the last step is making a decision. Even doing nothing can be a decision, and often that's where they ultimately decide to go.

To convince the buyer that you can help them on their journey—and that they should hire you to be their guide—they must believe that you know the shortest path to get them where they want to go. And you cannot possibly know the shortest path until you figure out where they are in their journey. That's the essential first step.

TRY THIS

- Be conversational. This involves a two-way dialogue that is geared toward helping the buyer solve a problem or get better.
- Listen to understand. Often, sellers can listen for what they want to hear. By listening to understand, we avoid happy ears.
- Show how you can help instead of telling.
- Make your emphasis on asking thoughtful questions instead of telling, explaining, or pitching.
- Visualize what it takes to purchase your product. Identify all the small steps that seem trivial.
- Create an impeccable first impression that really shows you care and understand them.

CHAPTER 2

ATTRACT, DON'T REPEL

HOW TO EARN TRUST BY PROJECTING CONFIDENCE

In my college years, I was attracted to the political arena. I majored in political science and was active in politics on and off campus. I was drawn to the "what makes people tick" side of politics, and I thought it might be my career until I discovered sales and technology. But I still appreciate the intellectual and emotional parts of the subject to this day. I have also learned more about sales by borrowing concepts from other disciplines and adapting them to my work in sales.

One of the key overlapping concepts between the two disciplines is the idea of desperation. A great example of this occurred on February 2, 2016, when presidential hopeful Jeb Bush took the floor to give a Republican primary speech in New Hampshire. Jeb proceeded to deliver an impassioned monologue about foreign policy, in which he alluded to American strength and how he would lead differently. When he finished, the audience sat in stony silence until he begged them to "please clap." The clip immediately went viral. To date it has garnered millions of views on YouTube, and pundits had a field day with the plea. Shortly thereafter, Jeb dropped out of the race.

While the words "please clap" were not Jeb's downfall, they certainly signaled something much deeper—that he and his campaign were inherently weak. This statement didn't just signal a deep desperation in that moment, but it reflected upon him as a person, as a leader. We saw it in his words, in his debates, and in his pleas for support from his own supporters at his own event; this served as a representation of the larger dynamic going on within his campaign. That's the message that stuck with voters. That's the perspective we all had of Jeb in 2016.

Desperation is a voter repellant, but it is also a buyer repellant. That's because desperation is a *people* repellant.

Consider another example. In the 1984 presidential election, rumors were swirling around about the health of then-president Ronald Reagan. Supporters were concerned how this might affect his chances of reelection. Reagan exacerbated concerns over his health when, in the first televised debate with Democratic challenger Walter Mondale, he stumbled, slurred, and seemed to have difficulty recalling basic words and thoughts on multiple occasions. Afterward, the opposition pounced on the chance to criticize him, especially about his age and mental capacity for a second term. The Great Communicator was in dire straits.

Reagan redeemed himself in the second televised presidential debate, however. At one point, the moderator alluded to the youthfulness of President John F. Kennedy and how during the Cuban Missile Crisis the young president would stay awake for days on end with very little sleep. He then proceeded to ask Reagan how he might handle such situations given his age.

In response to the question, Reagan coolly replied, "I

will not make age an issue of this campaign. I am not going to exploit, for political purposes, my opponent's youth and inexperience."

The audience erupted into laughter—and so did Mondale.

With a simple joke delivered confidently, Reagan sucked the energy out of the room and more importantly the power out of the question. He turned a serious and damning accusation of a question into a triumphant and decisive moment that would define how the nation viewed him at the time he needed it most. Two weeks later, Ronald Reagan won in one of the biggest landslides in US presidential history.

MEET THE MOMENT

What do these two examples tell us about the campaigns and the men behind them? Whether popular perception was fact or fiction, the two words Jeb Bush uttered cast him as feeble and unelectable, and the two sentences Ronald Reagan delivered painted him as clever, witty, and strong. It's the words we use that illustrate the larger narrative for the buyer, or in these cases, the voters. Our words and actions are the ultimate reference points that give the world a glimpse into who we are.

These examples are direct lessons in what happens on the sales floor regularly. Whether it's our phrases, our attitude, or our mindset, we get in the headspace of "please buy," just like Jeb did with his "please clap" mindset. The "please buy" mindset is a desperate one. It's disempowering. It's a buyer repellant. The best sellers I have ever known don't get in this mindset because they don't need any one given sale. They can lose a sale because they are confident enough in themselves and their own system. More important, they have done the work to build the actual pipeline to get to their goals and don't rely exclusively on one deal or another. The effect of having the right habits, mindset, and systems in place means that these sellers create enough space with their buyers to take calculated risks. Sure, they want the deal and will do everything in their power to get it. But they don't *need* it. And precisely because they can lose this sale, because they aren't desperate, the probability of them losing the deal is far less because they aren't projecting insecurity into the deal.

The irony of them being able to lose a sale with any given prospect is that they can have more honest conversations about how they can and cannot help their buyer and what their products can and cannot do. It breathes more oxygen into the call. Because they aren't so fixated on the result, they can pick up on little details about the buyer and be more responsive moment by moment. This, somewhat counterintuitively, makes them more effective, and they have higher success and conversion rates than the desperate salesperson clinging to every sale for dear life. It reminds me of a saying from the fundraising world: "The best time to get money from venture capitalists is when you don't need it." Sounds bizarre, but it's true. Projecting confidence makes your organization more appealing to investors, and the same is true of buyers.

Desperation can also become a factor when we are trying to get promoted. Another favorite saying of mine on this topic is "Do the job you want before you have it." The moral here is the same as in the fundraising example: if you want a job, the best way to stand out from the applicant pool is to start taking on responsibilities and showing competence before you actually have the job. A desperate approach is to hope for the job. The confident approach is to have a strong bias for action—to *do* something about it. For example, if you are in an entry-level sales role, start listening to sales calls, scoring them, and doing practice roleplays on your own. There are no rules preventing you from being proactive. The best bridge to what you want is not hope—it's construction. Construct what you want piece

Does this person seem like other confident people I have encountered before?

by piece, and what once seemed impossible suddenly seems accessible.

My only caveat to this rule is to make sure you're excelling in the role you're currently in before you attempt to get another.

LOOK THE PART

Confidence or desperation can come through not only in what we say but also in our demeanor. The first thing people notice about us is our tone on calls. I have heard countless pieces of advice on this topic, most of which I have discarded. I always recommend people take an even-keeled approach to tone and demeanor, almost matter-of-fact and confident. Having a clear command of the facts is one of the best ways to project confidence without the need for fluff. The second is our body language and facial expressions—these tap into the emotional piece. Subconsciously, our buyers evaluate us with every single interaction: *Does this person seem like other confident people I have encountered before?*

One of the biggest lessons in how to get better at sales is this: when it pertains to our demeanor with buyers, come from a place of equals. Too often I see salespeople acquiesce to every prospect demand or, worse, allow themselves to be treated as less than because they are the ones selling. Not only should we avoid doing this out of respect for ourselves, but it also hurts our sales efforts. If you know your product actually helps people get better, there should be no qualms about selling it or asking for their business. And under no circumstances should we allow others to treat us in a heated, rude, or disrespectful way just because they are a prospect or customer.

It also means we come to the table as adults and thus treat the buyer as an adult too. People can pick up on our emotions and thinking. If we are too deferential to others during the buying cycle, it can hurt our ability to help them. Once we come to the table as equals, we get to a place where we are on the exact same side. It becomes difficult to remove obstacles from the buying process if we ourselves are an obstacle—if our demeanor and lack of confidence get in the way of giving the buyer great experiences. The only way to get better at this is to practice with intention.

Another form of desperation is *hard selling*, or high-pressure selling, like the furniture salesperson in the introduction. She "needed" the sale and looked past what my partner and I wanted, parading us around the store to see what she thought we wanted instead of asking simple questions to understand what we were looking for. Through a question or two, she could have figured out that I was just about to quit my job and therefore was on a budget. Or that I had something clear in my mind that would propel us to purchase. Her tactics were old-school, ones that sellers would deploy to get buyers to give in to their will, often whether they needed the product or not. They place our own desire to hit a number over a prospective client's need to solve a problem. Selling doesn't mean we don't ever ask anyone to buy or that we never hold buyers accountable, but it means we don't pressure them to do things that they don't want to do. We facilitate the sale through meaningfully solving problems, removing obstacles from the buying process, and demonstrating confidence.

Another common area where confidence tends to fade is at the very end of a sales call. The salesperson will start the call hopeful, bright-eyed, and optimistic. Then throughout the call maybe they encounter resistance. By the end of the call they might feel overwhelmed, and they can often lose sight of the positivity they had when they entered the call. Maintaining that even-keeled, positive tone and demeanor throughout our sales calls helps get us in the right mindset to move past buyer concerns. I always like to save a bit of extra time at the end of a call specifically for this exercise—getting on the same page, addressing concerns, and spending lots of time with what I call "viewing behind the curtain," or understanding the facts, power dynamics, and motivations of the people in the organization we are trying to sell to beyond our champion (the person whom we are leveraging from the buyer's side to help us sell). Figuring out what goes on behind the curtain is realizing the organizational dynamics that can help or hurt any given deal. Maintaining confidence throughout can help open doors you didn't know you had.

Have you ever noticed how powerful people speak in group settings? Often, it's very direct. They use few words, and they often convey exactly what they mean. If someone is speaking to a buyer and uses the fewest possible words to convey their exact point, what does that convey to the buyer? Confidence. The most common example of this in a sales cycle is around delivering price. Many new sellers say the price and instead of letting it stand for itself they get insecure. "But don't worry, we can discount it for you," someone said to me recently, without giving me a chance to process the price they gave. Using fewer words and pausing are your friends—they are extensions of a confident mindset.

"Here it is." Then just allow them to fill the space.

If we offer up a price for a product and they have objections, that's not a bad thing. It just means we're getting to the truth faster, not that we can't sell.

PULL BUYERS TOWARD YOU, DON'T PUSH THEM AWAY

In helping our buyers make a purchase, we can push them toward the sale with a high-pressured approach, or we can pull them toward us. The only way we can pull buyers toward us is if they feel that we are in it for them—that we understand. If they get even the slightest hint that we're in it for ourselves, whether it be a commission or just the sale itself, they will be more reluctant to do business with us, or not engage at all. This is often a big reason for prospects and customers ghosting us or being unresponsive.

A common way this plays out is when a seller is pushing for a sale before the buyer has solved a problem. Even when we do find a problem, we often pounce on them. Finding a problem alone is *not enough*. Buyers must want to *do something* about this problem. Also, how big of a problem is this relative to all their other problems and priorities? Are they even aware of the problem? It might be an *issue* for them, but ranked against all their other problems, it's quite low. The question to ask yourself is whether they will *take action* on a problem.

Instead of a quick sell, what's needed when you bump up against your first problem that a buyer might be experiencing is more thoughtful discovery. First, you'll need to uncover how they feel about the problem on an emotional level. Many people might not see the so-called problem you've identified as a significant issue. So in this case, if you were to jump straight into sell mode, you and your prospect would be out of alignment. You're essentially pitching in the dark.

Get them to open up about the problem. My favorite way to do this is to ask them to show or explain their issue to you. When the discussion is purely intellectual, it's easy to hide and say, "Everything is fine." But when they show you the status quo, it becomes an entirely different story because (a) you can see their emotion toward the status quo; and (b) it serves as a powerful motivational tool.

Showing is crucial because it's experiential for both you and the prospect. If a prospect shows you some archaic process their company has, it becomes difficult to hide from that fact. They also re-experience their own negative emotions toward this process. It makes the abstract concrete.

Think about that for a moment. If you talk *about* what they do versus them *showing you* what they do, which will be more motivational? Often just by doing this you can motivate someone to *take action* on their own.

We seldom realize it, but we can get used to things that are bad for us. I can get used to eating cake every night after dinner and never change my behavior, despite the weight I've gained. But maybe I come to realize that I also want that summer body come July for the vacation I want to go on. That vacation is aspirational. Aspiration is hugely helpful for change, but alone it may not completely change behavior. I want to look great on the beach, sure, but I haven't changed my cake-eating behavior to get there. So, one thing I try to do for myself to change this behavior is to document it via a food journal; then I can become more aware of what I am eating. Imagine if my doctor asked me to show this to her. It creates *awareness* and *motivation* for change. If you want to attract people to you, get them to show you something that they are not showing all the other vendors on their short list.

Getting the prospect to show you the status quo might leave a typical salesperson salivating, but sales is about asking questions to get to root causes of problems. So, where a novice might jump straight into problem-solving mode, a seasoned seller knows to keep asking questions. Questions that breathe oxygen into our sales calls.

"Walk me through how x affects y."

"Can you show me how xyz would work in this specific scenario?"

"How would it work if we did x or y?"

The key is to go for detail and get a complete picture. This engages your prospect on a deeper emotional level than the other, surface-level sales conversations they are simultaneously having with other vendors. You'll come across as more thoughtful than your competitors. Now the buying experience becomes more attentive instead of surface level.

THE THREE THRESHOLDS

Motivation is your biggest friend in sales. And to get that motivation, we must cross three thresholds:

1. **The experiential threshold**—How do their past experiences impact the deal?
2. **The emotional threshold**—How do they feel emotionally about the deal?
3. **The logical threshold**—How will they build a logical case for the deal?

The *experiential threshold* references their own experiences with you, your product, and your company, and how you approach the problem that you are trying to solve relative to their past experiences. They evaluate you against their previous ordeals and see if this fits the "does this make sense" test. People's own experiences govern how they view the world, especially when it comes to sales. With so many data points to go from and so much information in the world, we often rely on our own experiences and make decisions based on these even in the face of data that says otherwise, simply from feeling overwhelmed.

An experience can be as small as what someone—say, another buyer—told you. It can be you having a bad experience with a vendor, so you rule out ever using them, or even a whole category of products. We are so closely tied to our personal experiences. They serve as the ultimate reference point that shapes our view of the world. To progress any sale, we have to overcome any negative experiential barriers to buying.

For example, I know a small-business owner who didn't realize that optimizing the messaging on her website and putting in a tool to help with conversion would strongly impact her business in a positive way. She just thought if she had a quality product, that would be good enough. Her experiences prior to this said the more she tweaked the class schedule, brought in high-quality teachers, and iterated on the product, the more students would come. After making that small change to her website, her business tripled in one month. Her initial experience of tweaking the product was replaced with delivering a high-quality product *and* making it easy for people to become customers. Now she has a new paradigm that shapes how she views her business. She started paying attention to *leads* and *students*.

The experience threshold is very closely tied to the emotional one. The *emotional threshold* goes deeper than just the buyer's experiences, though. It uncovers their attitudes, feelings, and emotions during a deal. It's the emotional motivation behind why someone chooses to work with you or not. Do they feel certain that you can help them? Have you uncovered deep frustrations? Is what you're saying a "nice to have" or a "need to have"? What are their attitudes on specific issues? Will they go to bat for you behind closed doors? How will the deal impact their reputation? Most of all, will what you're discussing compel them to act—to actually do something?

All these questions surround the fact that sales is more emotional than logical—by far. The emotional threshold is also the most important of the three, and without it a deal cannot be accomplished.

Finally there's the *logical threshold*. Once buyers are in a place where they see the value and are with you, it's time for them to make the case to others—and they do this through logical argumentation. Maybe the CFO is going to come in and try to cancel the deal because of economic concerns. Maybe revenue operations doesn't want to implement yet another tool. There is still emotion involved when selling to people beyond your initial contact in an organization, but the logical case is built to justify the emotional one, often at the highest levels of decision-making. What is the return on investment (ROI)? How does this solve acutely painful problems? How does this help me avoid catastrophe? How does this boost productivity or cut costs? The logical threshold is the nuts and bolts, the "makes sense on paper" justification for your tool. The ROI, the sound business case, the documentation, and more.

Pausing is your friend when you're strategizing, speaking, and selling in the context of these three thresholds. How does the buyer feel about this problem? How does it impact their business relative to other problems? Why are they using the product to begin with? What do they like about it, and what don't they like? Use this time to gain a firm understanding of not just the problem, but all the minute details surrounding said problem, most importantly how it affects their business and how they feel about it. They must want to *do* something about it. (Please do not ask prospects, "What impact will this have on your business?" as it comes across as canned.)

Once they have seen the light and noticed a problem, you will need to unpack the business ramifications. This is your connection from the emotional case in the earlier discovery to the logical case. The business case for your deal is usually the justification they make to others. Using logic is what helps you do this. By getting them to experience their own problems, then uncovering emotions around those problems, and finally connecting all of this to the more logical brain, you're setting yourself up for winning on three deeper levels of a buyer's psyche: the experiential case, the emotional case, and the logical case. You can also show a before and after of how they could use your product as a further motivator for sales success when building your case.

A question you might ask to learn more about the status quo is "Why wouldn't you just . . . ?" or "What makes you want to . . . ?" I generally avoid "why"-oriented questions because they can put buyers on the defensive, but in this scenario it works.

Let's say you're currently using a software product and I have a competing software product. If I am trying to get to the root cause of why you want to switch from your current provider to another, I can ask questions like these to get straight to it without being pushy. It's the opposite of what people expect. This question accomplishes another goal: getting buyers to reveal why they are doing research to begin with.

For example: "You mentioned you're using ACME for lead generation, and from the outside it seems like things are going OK. Why wouldn't you just keep using them?" This question works on specific feature comparisons as well, not just side-by-side product comparisons. The key, as with any question, is the delivery and tonality. This is the one exception to "why" questions.

Said differently, "Seems like everything is going fine with the product you're currently using. What makes you want to look into other options?"

Once you ask questions that pull the prospect toward you instead of pushing them away, it will completely change the dynamic of your sales calls and emails. I have had people who seemed against the software I was trying to sell who suddenly changed and completely opened up with this question.

PLANT THE SEED

We all know the more we push an idea, the more resistance we will get to that idea from other people. The more you tell someone to quit smoking, brush their teeth, or anything else, the more they will push back. People don't want their individual autonomy challenged. They want to feel like the idea is their own. Instead, plant a seed and let it flourish. Prime people to take action. Let them be the ones to reveal why they need something and also the ones who solve the problem. Let them be the hero of the story. Do anything except pressure them to your will.

People have long said that sales is more emotional than logical. But there's a small piece of the puzzle we leave out. To really think like a seller, we need to realize the buyer's perceptions and experiences. People's own experiences are the biggest reference point they have for understanding the world. So when we try to replace their experiences with our own, we are going to be met with resistance. Your experience of the world is that your product is amazing and everyone should buy it. The buyer's experience of the world is that it's a lot of work to implement and their reputation is on the line. Maybe they had a bad experience with your type of software. Maybe they understand how it all works already. Maybe they just have a couple of requirements they need met, and then they will fight for you—will really go to bat to get the deal across the line.

The point is we don't know unless we ask and discover. The point of discovery in sales is not to ask a bunch of invasive questions that make people feel weird. Discovery is meant not only to find the problem but also to understand the entire landscape around the problem, with the fewest possible questions asked to get there. Why do they do the things the way they do, and how does it impact their business? What are the human-level emotions around said problem? This can take minutes or years to accomplish. There's no set timeline, because every product, person, and company are different.

The point of discovery is to understand the motivation that will prompt them to take action. The biggest way to pull buyers toward you is to ask. The biggest way to push them away from you is to tell. Asking is like bringing together magnets that have different poles; they are instantly attracted to one another. Telling is like trying to shove together magnets with the same pole; they are repelled. This is the dynamic of asking versus telling in sales. Telling alienates our buyers and, just like with magnets, quite literally pushes them away from us.

GIVE OR TAKE

When buyers enter conversations with salespeople, they quickly register whether the person is giving or taking. Givers are the ones that lead with identifying and solving the buyer's problems. Takers apply pressure on the prospect to get the sale. Modern buyers have gotten very good at distinguishing between the two. This isn't to suggest that you act like a customer service representative, but rather that you help the customer achieve their business goals and objectives and that a side effect will be you gain a sale. This isn't about being passive or creating more work for yourself. It's about uncovering human motivation, figuring out what steps need to be taken, and getting others to go along with you to accomplish those steps.

Many sellers will follow up with buyers without any changes or meaningful updates. They take time without giving anything back. Say you are in a sales cycle with a seller, and you pause because of some internal problem you experience at your company. Most salespeople here simply follow up over and over with what feels like a "Ready to buy yet?" narrative without any meaningful exchange of new information. This never works because whatever has caused the buyer to pause to begin with hasn't been dealt with. So, either they overcome this obstacle on their own and reengage, or the seller figures out a way to help them through the obstacle so they can resume. Or worse, they never reengage, and the seller doesn't know why. What's needed most is an understanding of the root causes of the behavior.

A way to give in this situation is simply to understand. What is holding up your prospect? Even asking the question will help you so much more in gaining trust points. If they're not in market now, be the one they choose when they are. You have the benefit of having already spoken to them, a luxury that other salespeople might not have.

Another way to communicate that you are a giver is by telling a great story. Not in the smooth-talking salesperson way, but in a way that really resonates. Real, contextual stories that are relatable to your buyer. Become familiar with a wide array of customer stories at your company. Don't use generalized anecdotes to apply in every situation but rather specific ones that speak to specific problems a buyer is facing. One way people use stories is through social proof, in which you use examples, case studies, and anecdotes of how people or companies work with you as a tool to create a desire for others to work with you. The problem comes in when social proof feels unbelievable or not relatable. Use social proof from their same industry and business size: "Hey, I was actually working on this problem the other day . . . and they were just like you."

When most people prospect me, they compare my startup to how they work with Facebook, Google, and Apple. Sure, these are famous companies with household names, but the comparison misses the mark. They would be better off citing companies in my industry and around my size, with similar problems. I don't have the same problems as Facebook. Not even close.

Case studies and random marketing statistics that salespeople use tend to rank low on the persuasive scale for buyers as well. However, case studies can be very effective tools if they fit into the larger narrative of being hypercontextual. It's more that the way we currently use them is faulty than the idea itself being faulty. Creating meaningful case studies with buyers can also be a great way for them to become advocates for your product and help you deepen your relationships with them. There are tons of tools that help with this as well—and I recommend using tools to help with this.

SALES SHOULD BE FUN

In the old world of selling, sales calls would sound stiff, overly formal, and unrelatable. In the new world, buyers want to get problems solved quickly. But that doesn't mean our calls should be stale. People buy from people. Having light, friendly, and conversational calls with humor is important. It's OK to be funny and to use humor as well. That's encouraged!

It's the small things that really make a difference, like remembering to smile genuinely. Sales is really about energy transfer. So why not anchor this in your favor by starting it off with a soft, genuine smile? Also try to talk about things besides the weather, sports, or other boring topics at the top of the call (unless the buyer really cares about these things). Put something interesting on your desktop or virtual background that is a personal conversation starter. I used to have a picture of me bungee jumping as my desktop background. It prompted interesting conversations in nine out of ten sales calls.

It sounds simple, but starting every call on a positive,

casual note goes a long way. Good vibes are literally contagious. I used to put sticky notes on my desk to remind myself of this: "Remember to smile," one would say. Putting one to three sticky notes on your desk for the top skills you are working on at any given time seems mundane, but it can be helpful. It also reminds you to be conscious about a behavior. People need to be reminded more than they need to be told.

There are so many things we can do to lighten up our work and genuinely have fun. I once worked on a sales team where we'd have competitions for who could send the best personalized emails. One of the best emails I heard during this period was from a senior salesperson who wrote a poem for their buyer. Another rewrote a Justin Bieber song, but incorporated the buyer's pain points and how we solved them. Both of those instances resulted in meetings being booked with prospects, so humor can be effective too.

Having fun in an authentic manner is one of the best ways to portray confidence. It works well with buyers because it is human. Confidence is a magnet that pulls people toward us. But being genuinely confident is just part of what it takes to create impeccable sales experiences. We also need a magnifying glass to show us what buyers really care about.

TRY THIS

- Use fewer words to project confidence in your sales calls, especially when talking about price.
- Practice speaking in an even tone, with a strong command of the facts and a friendly demeanor.
- Practice using relevant case studies as opposed to broad-stroked, generalized ones.
- Show your buyer a compelling before-and-after example of using your product. Showing is often more powerful than telling.
- Get your buyer to show you their status quo for the problem they want to solve.
- Practice asking questions to help buyers realize what they need or want instead of simply telling them.
- Have fun with your calls and emails. Be playful and authentic.
- Keep up the confidence, especially at the end of a call or when concerns are brought up. This helps you and the buyer.

CHAPTER 3

PIECING IT TOGETHER

HOW TO UNDERSTAND WHAT REALLY MOTIVATES BUYERS TO ACT

I didn't know what was going on, but one of my salespeople was really mad at me.

Andrew's close rate had plummeted after his initial on-boarding. During his first three months as an employee (often referred to as a *ramp*), Andrew did so well. He was like a straight-A student with me. Then, at about the five-month mark, he started getting defensive.

"I don't know what else you want from me," he said.

I had to try not to laugh at that one, because what I was saying was to simply look at something objectively with me. In ramp mode, he was a great student and open to advice, but now that it was time to perform, he did not want any feedback. I was determined to work through this because I really believed in his potential. Sales coaches always look for "coachability," or how good someone is at receiving and implementing feedback, which I agree is a desirable and necessary trait of salespeople. But sometimes we forget that we all have human moments.

The issue I was trying to subtly show was that Andrew was rushing through the front part of the call and missing all the good stuff. He couldn't figure out how to help the prospect make a purchase, to go from buyers saying, "I have a problem" to "I want to do something about it with you." He didn't know why the customer wanted to buy our products to begin with. He didn't know why any of the customers had bought before, and it was hurting his close rate.

Let's soften the blow, I thought. "Why don't we swap places? I will be in the hot seat, and you can critique me."

I turned off the recording to his call and we did a roleplay. I let him be the customer, and I was the salesperson.

During my roleplay, I did a brief introduction and summarized what I already knew about the prospect and the problem they were looking to solve. I started by the giving the prospect plenty of space to talk about the problem. Then I stopped and we did an assessment of the roleplay. I asked Andrew to summarize it and provide feedback.

Andrew pointed out how overall the trajectory of the intro of the call went much smoother. He saw how getting right into the meat of the conversation was a better way to start instead of asking who the buyers were and what they did. He liked the idea of summarizing information you knew about them to build trust, not forcing them to repeat themselves. And he appreciated the use of a light agenda that gave context for what was to be expected on the call.

As we kept discussing his feedback, Andrew even brought up a few items that I hadn't thought of, which made both of us feel better—less like a manager and salesperson and more like two people looking at a problem on the same side and trying to solve it together. People are never the enemy in sales, problems are. And so in this exercise, he was able to get out of the mindset of feeling in the hot seat and see me as someone genuinely trying to help him. Andrew also calmed down a bit because he saw I was willing to literally put myself in his shoes. He described the experiences he was having on the phone with buyers via roleplay, and I acted as though I were him. This did wonders for improving trust between us. This is an important lesson for anyone who wants to be in sales management one day. Never ask someone to do a job you're unwilling to do yourself. If your career goals involve leading people, you don't necessarily have to be better than them, but you do have to show basic competence and a willingness to put yourself in their shoes.

There were three main takeaways from this experience:

1. When trying to improve, focus on the biggest issues, one at a time. Don't try to improve everything all at once.
2. Ask others to roleplay. Switching up the roles a little bit can help you get out of a temporary rut or setback.
3. When helping others (for those of you that might want to help lead a team), be prepared to be vulnerable yourself.

A week later, once Andrew nailed the intro of the call, we got into the meat of what I wanted to work on: figuring out how to get him to progress a deal by finding the buyer's *why*.

THE THREE WHYS

Applying these lessons, I created a simple framework I like to use for scoring sales calls, which I call the *three whys*:

1. Find their why.
2. Demo their why.
3. Progress their why.

The framework is simple but extremely powerful.

FIND THEIR WHY

This is where the concept of the emotional threshold we talked about in the previous chapter comes into play in a most pronounced way. Finding their why is not the ROI your tool can provide. It's usually that deep-seated, acutely painful, or even deeply desired place the buyer wants to be. Finding their why is about going deep.

Finding someone's why does not mean asking them why. A why question can put us on the defensive because it forces us to justify ourselves. Rather, we want to *reveal* their why through asking other types of questions. I always recommend people read the book *Never Split the Difference* by Chris Voss to improve this specific skill. This book is foundational to any sales team.

Finding their why means uncovering the emotional drivers of our buyers that will spring them into action—their motivation. It also might not be immediately top of mind for the prospect. Finding the buyer's why is the most difficult part of the process for sellers. It's difficult for two reasons: we get happy ears, and it takes enormous skill and trust to get the buyer to show their cards. Most salespeople pounce too early. Most whys never get revealed.

For example, let's say you are selling a service that helps startups with compliance. Previously, we spoke about the need to be different. Hopefully you've written down a compelling reason you're different from your competitors. Some companies provide this in the form of battlecards—essentially digital

51

Finding their why means uncovering the emotional drivers of our buyers that will spring them into action—their motivation.

index cards that list how we win against specific competitors. Battlecards can be helpful for sure.

But what about on a more emotional level? What is the one thing your buyer needs with compliance that no one else can figure out? A lot of people gravitate to price. Sure, sometimes price can make a difference. Some people focus on differentiators alone. Being different can make a difference. But it is their *why* that compels people to act.

So, thinking deeper here. What is their why? What could their why be?

Maybe their why is some small technicality. I've seen people buy products because of a simple integration that competitors didn't offer. Maybe it's being easy to use. I've seen a terrible user experience be the reason people choose to leave vendors and flock to new ones. Maybe it's peace of mind. I had a friend pay off an entire mortgage just so he wouldn't have to think about it, even though he said he knew he could have used that money to earn more over the long run. Maybe it's just not doing some little frustrating thing that a competitor is known for doing. Maybe it's showing off in front of their boss so they can get promoted. Most of the time it's a pain point they have but may not even be aware of when you speak to them.

Pain points alone are great, but their existence does not guarantee a sale. People must think, believe, and feel that doing something about a pain point is urgent, helpful, or desired. They must want to take action on it. Finding their why picks up where the pain point leaves off. It's not just about a little bit of pain—after all, humans are adaptable, even to things that might not be good for us.

Most people call the top half of a sales call *discovery*, which is accurate. But discovery shouldn't be a laundry list of questions. It also shouldn't be limited to any particular point in time. Discovery is ongoing and has no end point. Discovery then becomes synonymous with uncovering human motivation on experiential, emotional, and logical levels.

DEMO THEIR WHY

Once you find their why, you want to really stick to that. Sometimes we like to put our own narrative, our own "this makes sense to me," into a deal. So often, projecting our own views can be damaging if they are not aligned with the buyer's. We start showing more than we need to because we know our product is great and we want to share it with the world. But there is an important dynamic to note here.

For example, say you are selling a computer. If a buyer comes in and wants a computer that is great for writing, you should show them the parts of the product that relate just to that. If they are a writer, you don't need to show them how they can play computer games. It sounds silly, but this dynamic is more the rule than the exception.

The more you get away from their why, a computer that is great for writing, the larger the price seems as a result. Features make people think about price. Features people don't want or need make buyers think that the price is too steep. "Well, I only need it for this, I don't need all that other stuff, so how much would it be for *just* this?"

Don't show too much. It's common to want to show everything you can do, no matter the product. It doesn't matter if it's a house or software. That doesn't mean you can't ever show extra features or highlight things you think the buyer might be interested in, but it does mean you should confirm. People generally have their requirements they want met, and the rest can be noise. When you highlight the noise, it leads to confusion and frustration—it can even come across as not listening. It can also draw attention to your competitor or even create extra work. Once you find their why, craft the narrative of the rest of your conversation around that. If you think another part of your product might make sense to them, preface it before diving in.

"I know you mentioned that the most important part of this software was that the admin work for your team was minimal; I think there's a couple more pieces we might look at as well. If I am wrong, no worries—we can move on—but I thought I'd at least give you the option to check out a few more pieces of the tool." Boom. We make them feel in control and we lose no steam if they say no, but we still keep the narrative around their why.

Only demo what you must. Do not demo the entire product if you don't have to.

PROGRESS THEIR WHY

Progressing their why is about building consensus to get a deal across the finish line. It's linking up with your buyer, arm in arm, and then peering beyond the curtain into the organization.

Spend. Time. Here.

Top performers I have worked with in my career spend much more time outlining and planning for next steps than do middle and low performers. They are also much more specific.

Think about it for a second. Let's take any goal you want to accomplish. Let's say you take pen and paper and write down this goal. That's good. It's a step. Now let's say you visualize completing it. Then let's say you write down all the little steps it would take to actually complete the goal. Then you write down the who, what, where, when, why, how of that goal. It's not enough for buyers to say they want something anymore. We, as sellers, must help them visualize and project manage to completion. In the same way we can improve goal setting by being specific, we can improve next steps and how a deal progresses.

At the "progress their why" step of the framework, we should be asking not, "How are we going to win this deal?" but "How are we going to lose it?" When we say how we will win a deal, we often go into happy ears mode. When we ask how we will lose it, we automatically highlight the areas of weakness that we can then correct for before they actually become a problem. You should be able to answer that question for every deal in your pipeline. This helps you psychologically to create an airtight narrative across your pipeline and stay one step ahead of your buyers and manager alike. Then when your manager asks you, "How are you going to win this deal?" you'll have your checklist, because you have visualized, thought through obstacles, and started to set a project management plan in motion with your champion.

The biggest takeaway here: If you leave it up to chance, it will favor the status quo. If you leave it up to the status quo, the deal will lean away from you rather than toward you. I like to control for chance.

So instead, we should get in the mindset of project management. Envision all the microsteps that closing a deal entails, and work backward from there. This usually involves being very proactive about who is involved and what they need to see, but also anticipating blockers. If there are blockers to deals, how can you get those concerns out of the way up front? If certain actors are blockers, will that impede you from winning the deal, or will it just dampen the deal's momentum? Don't get to the end of the call, get off the phone, and leave things up to chance. Try to control the controllable without trying to control people. Focus on the variables and obstacles and go from there. I highly recommend using both account plans and mutual action plans here. It is incredibly difficult to manage a pipeline while keeping all this information in your head. Then when you do show up for follow-up calls, you'll have the information on hand. Trying to pull it from memory is simply too hard for anyone.

If you're feeling extra ambitious, try tracking your attendance rates to calls after your first interaction with someone. Measuring call-attendance rates from first call to second is a good indicator of how the prospect is feeling. High no-show rates on the second call, the follow-up call, are an indicator that something wasn't quite right on that first call. An even better one is whether they are taking the proper steps on their end to get the deal done. Watch for actions as opposed to always listening for words.

WORKING BACKWARD FROM THE BUYER

At the top of the chapter, my feedback to Andrew wasn't "Hey, you sound like a robot" but rather a longer exercise in trying to find the root cause of why he sounded so great during onboarding but then plateaued and plummeted once he was "on the sales floor." We started from that root cause and worked backward to tonality and how he was handling his sales calls, his delivery. Once we fixed the top of the call, we were able to get to the next-biggest problem he was encountering, which concerned how he conducted discovery. This took weeks to improve.

Crafting the sale is about detaching from the internal craving to earn a sale just enough so we can create the space to focus on the details that matter most. One of those details is working backward from the buyer. What is the optimal buying experience for them? How can I remove obstacles to the buying process for them? What are the customer's objectives? How are they trying to accomplish these?

This doesn't mean taking a passive approach to sales. We still have quotas to hit, after all. It means not being so eager to get the sale that we alienate the buyer and ignore important steps along the way.

Let's take a look at how we might handle a situation as simple as a buyer asking a question.

What if they ask, "How does that part of the tool work?"

In this scenario, it's easy to just explain and keep going. But after you have adequately answered, pause briefly and ask about the significance of the question. What you want to establish is why they asked it.

So first, explain in a succinct way how that part of the tool works. Then ask something like this:

"How is that important to you?"

"What part of that stands out the most?"

Now you have explained what they wanted to know and figured out why they wanted to know it, which helps you create a better sales experience for them.

Now let's go back and handle an actual "objection."

"I don't think your tool will have the right ROI for the investment we make," the buyer protests.

When they've posed an objection like this, it's important to walk them through how the product works because it means they are not with you. Any time someone brings up a concern or objection, you must do four things:

1. **Isolate the concern.** When you isolate it, you can almost detach it from the rest of the conversation so you can deal with it.
2. **Resolve.** Resolve it or you can't go back to the regular conversation.
3. **Confirm.** Confirm that this issue is resolved.
4. **Redirect.** Now you can redirect back to the conversation.

The only exception here is if the concern is too large for this call and you need additional time or help, but as a rule of thumb this strategy works eight out of ten times.

Too often, unresolved concerns end up being major sticking points further in negotiations. Without being too eager, gently resolve concerns earlier on, before they become cemented in the customer's or prospect's mind.

"I appreciate you highlighting that concern," you answer. "Earlier you mentioned you have twenty inbound leads per month. On average, we're seeing a 60 to 70 percent higher conversion without our product."

Then take the time to walk this buyer through the math. Show them what the potential ROI could be based on your experience with other buyers. Discover exactly where the math does not add up for them. Correct this before going back to the overarching conversation.

AMBIGUITY IS A GOOD THING

I think a lot of salespeople would struggle with the simplicity of the three-whys framework, particularly because it leaves room for some ambiguity. People don't like ambiguity. We want answers. But we already know that our buyers are not all the same and their problems certainly are not. So, this allows for the buyer to be different as well as the seller. It gives us space to be responsive and adaptive instead of overly prescriptive.

Do I still set a very light agenda on my calls? Of course. Do I still try to close the deal? Absolutely. Do I still use concepts from an array of sales books? Yes. But I remove the rigidity of having to use the same process every time, and in doing so I try to create more space for understanding. This framework also gives me the space to respond to social cues and the needs of the moment. Some people call this *situational awareness,* which I am a huge proponent of. The results have been astounding for people I've worked with who have used this type of thinking. The level of thoughtful conversations I have had with sales teams using a framework like this has moved us from the world of sales drones to sales thinkers and creative problem solvers. The latter produce results and drive revenue.

I always strongly advocate for salespeople to have peer-to-peer training sessions, both in the form of call-recording training and by introducing new sales concepts and then workshopping and roleplaying them to anchor performance. I've found peer-led feedback sessions to be among the most useful activities any salesperson can do—yet so few take advantage of them. Many people trade the discomfort of listening to their own voices for top performance. There's a certain pride in self-sufficiency that you can build by doing this sort of activity—pride in knowing that you can score your own calls with your team and get better on your own.

Many of the salespeople I have spoken to want to be in some sort of leadership position, whether that be VP of sales, account management, or even entrepreneurship (although I think we need to normalize those who choose to stay in individual contributor sales roles for the duration of their career). Getting really good at identifying the one area that you can improve on and then relentlessly focusing on that until it has actually improved is a great way to take ownership and set your own path for your future goals. This is a strong skill for helping to move entire teams forward as well. Don't let the discomfort of growth dissuade you from being more successful and making more money. Create a simple scorecard, and then set up time with a peer to score each other's calls twice a month. After a short while, you will be the one everyone goes to for advice.

DRILL FOR PERFECTION

Think about what happens in volleyball if you drill, or repeatedly practice a serve. Repeatedly practicing the motion is essential so that once you're in a game, you've got it down pat. If the only time you ever practice is during a game, you won't improve nearly as fast or as far. What's required is practice on one skill at a time outside a live-action game to get better. This is true of any sport or skill you're looking to develop. Drilling is what you do to get better at any skill outside of sales, but many times its power is overlooked in the business world. Sure, the live-action game helps, too, but practicing alongside it is crucial.

One of my favorite phrases I heard growing up was "Practice doesn't make perfect, perfect practice makes perfect." I think this starts with a drill on a specific subset, or microskill, that is honed to perfection, and then you move on to the next most critical skill. This is how I went from no revenue on the board to top performer in a Fortune 500 company in one quarter. It's also the same way I scaled a startup from less than $1 million in revenue to a nine-figure valuation. By applying those microskill lessons to entire teams, you can level up an entire organization.

TRY THIS

- Create a simple framework that works for you when you're listening to calls. Borrow mine or invent your own. Then create a scorecard for sections and rate yourself and others from 1 to 10. Provide space on the scorecard for qualitative notes as well. Email me if you need help on this: michael@callypso.io.

- Set aside time to peer-review calls at least twice per month.

- Focus first on the one skill that, if improved, would most enhance your performance. Drill this skill and then move on to the next one.

- Take notes when listening back to your calls. It's hard to remember all the dynamics that unfold. When you take meaningful notes on what was said that went well and what didn't go so well, it helps you provide more actionable feedback to yourself and others.

- Rate your calls. Don't just say it went well or poorly. On a scale of 1 to 10, how well do you think you did? Why? Over time, you'll start understanding why you give scores the way you do. If you're already doing this, eliminate the number 7 so it forces you to give a more concrete number. A 7 can often be a gray area, whereas a 6 or 8 signals "needs improvement" or "not looking so bad."

CHAPTER 4

ONE SIZE DOES NOT FIT ALL

HOW TO SOUND LIKE A HUMAN BEING, NOT A ROBOT

In 2019, I got a free ticket to a big company's sales confer-ence in San Francisco. I was living in the city at the time, so I dropped by. One of the sessions that caught my eye was a talk by Joe Terry, then-CEO of VantagePoint, called "Why Sales Methodologies Are Failing."

I expected this session was going to be about which sales methodologies were the best, most modern, and recom-mended for use, but it ended up being a bit different from that. What Joe and his team demonstrated, and what their research supported, was that the top sellers didn't singularly subscribe to one methodology over another—they subscribed to many. More specifically, Joe and his team posited that top salespeo-ple applied the right methodology at the right time.

Joe's talk was immensely valuable to me for a few reasons. The first was that he used data from real, tangible studies to support what I had noticed for years through managing sales teams. As a manager of hundreds and hundreds of salespeople over my career, I knew that the top performers adapted their tactics depending on the moment, as opposed to running the same play over and over in varying situations.

But unfortunately, this is not what I have observed at most organizations. Most companies teach a rinse-and-repeat model to their sales teams. They usually pick a broadly used methodology, zone in on that, train the entire team, then hold the team accountable to using it. The mindset of sales leadership becomes "Just follow the process" without tangible and thoughtful explanations of *how* salespeople can improve or even if different situations require different approaches.

CONNECTING THE DOTS

I once had a salesperson who was booking a ton of meetings and closing a large volume of deals and then plateaued. I sat with him and observed him one afternoon to see what he was doing differently, and finally I asked him, "What do you think you're doing differently now versus before?" He mentioned that a manager had walked over and told him to stop selling a certain way and instead follow that manager's process. I explained to him that the strategies and tactics he was using before were fine to use. He was simply using a slight variation of a methodology that worked for him. I asked him to try his old way of doing things for a week. His results immediately went back up.

I never understood what managers meant when they used vague phrases like "Just add value." That's like telling a person learning how to box to "punch better." Well, duh! I know if I am not sparring well that I need to "punch better." But maybe I need to keep my hands up to guard my face. Maybe I should use a certain hook more often than a jab. Maybe I can duck more as well. Don't just tell me *what* to do. Tell me *how* to do it: What specifically can I improve on? How might I slightly tweak what I am doing? What part of my call needs improvement? It's easier to ask people to follow a preset logical, step-by-step process than to take the time to properly diagnose a specific problem and offer solutions in a very contextual way. The next time someone tells you what to do and you're confused, don't be afraid to ask how to do it. The best managers will help connect the dots.

Back at the conference in San Francisco, I called my CEO and eagerly struck up a conversation on the session I had just attended. We had already decided to ditch teaching one singular methodology to our sales team in favor of a more flexible model where we taught many, so I knew he was very interested in the topic. We had a long conversation about why canned sales approaches were fading away. The days of hard trial closes were over. (A *trial close* is when you ask someone if they will buy a product before showing it to them. For example, "If I show you this printer and it does everything you say you need, will you buy it today?") Being adaptive means that you learn multiple methodologies, apply the right one at the right time, and use multiple tools to sell. I also think there's tremendous value in learning about many methodologies. Then you can treat them like tools in a toolbox as opposed to one singular process you follow.

My favorite analogy here is a lesson we can borrow from the medical industry. A doctor who practices patient-centered care is tremendously involved in centering everything about diagnosis, treatment, procedures, and so on around the patient themselves. When sales managers teach this to their teams, the salespeople are way more equipped at providing better sales experiences for their customers, which in turn creates more favorable outcomes for everyone.

Let's talk about what Joe Terry was not saying, though. He

never said, "Do whatever you want," which is how I think some people would interpret his words at first glance. The research implies that top sellers are highly skilled at knowing when to use what tool, not that they cycle through different tools at random.

What Joe and the research he cited found was that people with poor results applied no methodology at all. People who had average results used a singular methodology, while top performers used many. They were well versed in all kinds of different methodologies and applied the right one at the right time. This was more than "I just want to do it my way," which is what sales managers frequently hear on the sales floor. This was "I want to do the right thing for the moment because that's what yields results."

Knowing when to apply the right methodology, or using situational awareness, is also helpful to the buyer. If you are trying to do a long-drawn-out discovery session using a new methodology you learned when all the person wants to do is buy, you are making the process harder for your buyer. The same is true if someone doesn't have enough information and needs more time before closing. Deploying the right message through the right methodology at the right time is key to success. This is where salespeople can quickly go from OK performance to changing income brackets.

ONE-SIZE-FITS-ALL METHODOLOGIES

I started on the journey to understand sales methodologies long before that day in San Francisco, though; it began when I attended a presentation on the book *The Challenger Sale* by Matthew Dixon and Brent Adamson. The training was given by one of my mentors, and I furiously took notes. The next month we practiced the concepts we learned from the book, which gave me a newfound sense of confidence. My sales numbers were decent before the training, but now they were excellent.

In *The Challenger Sale*, Dixon and Adamson break salespeople down into five different types, with their central claim being that the "challenger" is the best type of salesperson. According to the authors, the challenger is provocative and teaches or challenges the customer to see things from a new perspective. The idea is that they show the customer something they didn't know about their business.

The methodology laid out in *The Challenger Sale* is taught all over the world and has helped countless salespeople, me included. There's just one small problem with it: It doesn't work in every scenario. In fact, it can be counterproductive. I've experienced that firsthand.

But *The Challenger Sale* helped me in this moment because I was very new to sales and was at the lowest confidence level of my career. I needed the confidence boost that the teaching provided to help me speak to business owners in a way that would garner their trust and respect. The problem came months or years later, when I would try to apply this methodology to all sales situations. Once I had the confidence, the "challenging" aspect started to backfire a bit. I literally lost a deal one time because I did not want to budge on a concern the buyer had. My manager pulled me aside later and said, "I know very well you could have closed that deal." I slowly learned that not every buyer needs to be challenged. In fact, most people in today's world need the opposite—a positive sales experience matters more than ever. Balancing this fact with the real boost the methodology gave to my confidence as a new seller was critical.

One of the problems I frequently encounter with salespeople is that when you teach them a methodology, they sound very scripted. This was the original reason I started to depart from teaching methodologies as an early step in onboarding.

No matter what I did, people would still come across as inorganic and canned. More importantly, the buyers were picking up awkward vibes. When I switched to teaching sales concepts from an array of methodologies, results improved.

On the topic of scripting, I've heard many people say things like, "The best actors in the world use a script." The best actors in the world are also in controlled environments and can have do-overs if their tonality is off or they execute the script improperly—a luxury salespeople are not afforded.

As mentioned earlier, I am a huge fan of Chris Voss's *Never Split the Difference*. Even though the book does not technically offer a methodology, it will help you up your game with negotiation and selling in general. This should be required reading for anyone in a customer-facing role. The key for me in teaching the concepts from this book was to workshop them using real examples from my own company. This was hugely valuable instead of simply reading the book and moving on.

There are also books outside the realm of sales that are extremely useful to salespeople. One of the very best is James Clear's *Atomic Habits*. This is one of the finest books on creating a system of success for yourself rooted in habits and consistency. Books on psychology are often quite helpful as well. I'm a fan of Daniel Kahneman's *Thinking, Fast and Slow*, but there are others as well. Jeb Blount's *Fanatical Prospecting* is great for any seller, but I have especially given this book to people who are new to sales or in sales development, full-time prospecting roles.

One of the main takeaways for me was to give salespeople an array of tools at their disposal so they can be more agile in the selling process. Agility, adaptiveness, reading the buyer, and situational awareness are all areas of critical importance to getting top results.

SYSTEMS FOR THE WIN

If you had to choose who was better at selling based on the following statements, who would you go with?

Salesperson A: I am the best at adhering to mandated sales methodologies.

Salesperson B: I have the best system of anyone on my team.

I'd go with B.

Having a great system speaks to the microhabits that encompass sales—the consistency piece. It's getting the little things right that aggregate to make up the sum of all parts. Here are some of my tools/systems for selling:

- System #1—Note-taking as a tool for active listening
- System #2—Calendar blocking sacred time
- System #3—Hygiene
- System #4—Perfect practice, not just practice, makes perfect
- System #5—Pipeline coverage

Let's take them one by one.

SYSTEM #1—NOTE-TAKING AS A TOOL FOR ACTIVE LISTENING

Most salespeople I know take notes to get qualifying criteria, to update next steps, or to capture basic information. These are all necessary for selling, but you can go much further. Very few use note-taking as a tool for active listening. Proper note-taking helps you go so much further by capturing the true motivation that the ear alone can have a hard time discerning. Whether you're listening back to calls, participating in a role-play, or on live calls with prospects and customers, use note-taking to nail discovery.

Here are a few ways to go further with note-taking:

a. **Create a note template that works for you on different types of calls.** A call with someone you have never spoken to should be different from your sixth call with someone.

For a brand-new call, I always capture the following:

- Qualifying information
- Pain/problems
- Tools they are using
- Their role
- Other actors
- Their motivation for change
- Next steps

For a call where I have already spoken to the person, I capture all the above, plus the following:

- Where we left off last call
- What needs to happen next
- Potential blockers

What if you print sheets of paper with the items on the list above? Then you can give your mind a bit of space to focus on what the buyer is actually saying, because you already have what you need to capture on paper. Showing up to calls with this type of document reviewed and in hand can make a big difference;

you'll be fully present enough to capture and do something about the most important parts of a call. The worst salespeople I know show up to calls unprepared, ready to reflexively respond to any- and everything. Unpreparedness results in ill fortune for people in revenues roles.

b. **Draw connections.** I circle and draw connections to things that work together as well as information that doesn't seem to fit. For instance, if they mention a tool, but then they also mention a tool that has duplicative functionality, I might dig in to learn why that is the case. Or if they mention at the top of the call an item that is inconsistent with a point they make toward the end of the call, I can lightly explore gaps and go to deeper levels of discovery.

c. **Write with pen and paper.** I always write with pen and paper, and then I type my notes on the computer right after the call. Writing helps me remember and connect with the information better. The combination of writing and then entering details in the computer enables me to reinforce what was said and not forget, set any follow-ups right then and there, and also get out any material the call requires. I try never to go more than a few hours before entering the information into the computer.

SYSTEM #2—CALENDAR BLOCKING SACRED TIME

Calendar blocking is a way of saying, "This time is sacred." Don't block time and then move it. In my experience, the first thing to get moved when a conflict arises is prospecting time.

When onboarding, I think it is especially important to calendar block and then figure out how to keep the habit when you ramp into the role. Try blocking your calendar and treating those blocks as sacred. Don't be afraid to make tweaks and adjustments, but when you're done, lock it in. This is hugely valuable for making sure you get everything done. For example, many sellers don't carve out time for prospecting. Then when they close out their pipeline, they find they have little to go from for the next week or month. Calendar blocking helps you get out in front of any problems. It's like taking your vitamins—it's proactively good for you and it prevents problems later.

An example of a calendar block I've frequently used is what some people in the industry call a *power hour*. This is a call block where you set a goal for what you want to accomplish in terms of activity and number of calls made, and then you complete that with the rest of your team in one hour's time. Using time blocks and goals together are easy ways to be more productive in sales. The thing you want to avoid is getting to the end of the day and not really remembering what you accomplished. If you start with a goal, you will know whether you hit it by the end of the day. If you want to go even further with this, have a team member you pair up with, virtually or in person, where you communicate goals as well as progress.

Here's a sample calendar block:

8–8:30 a.m.—Call prep and email correspondence

8:30–10:30 a.m.—Follow-up calls

10:30 a.m.–noon—Social and email selling

1 p.m.—Internal meeting block

2 p.m.—New prospect calls

3 p.m.—Prospecting and prep for the following day

Once you have blocked your calendar to your liking, the last detail I recommend adding to each block is a quantifiable goal. If it stays as a generic calendar block with no clear goal, the time can be wasted. If a goal is made clear, you're more likely to actually complete it.

So for the 2:00 p.m. "new prospect calls" block, for example, you would want to add a goal of fifteen calls or some attainable number for you to complete in that time. Different organizations emphasize different methods for outreach, so adjust your calendar accordingly.

SYSTEM #3—HYGIENE

The little things matter in sales. From updating the pipeline to keeping accurate data in your systems, top performers are often way ahead of their managers when it comes to hygiene. When salespeople are ahead of their managers when it comes to seemingly trivial but critical elements of sales, like updating the customer relationship management (CRM) tool, they can have more fruitful conversations with their managers. Imagine if time spent in conversations were on coaching and specific deals the salesperson is working on instead of "Why isn't this report updated?"

Let's go back to note-taking one more time, for example. It sounds boring, but it's hugely critical. Properly entering notes into your systems helps you stay on top of your business and make sure all your account data is up to date. When it comes to hygiene and, in this case, note-taking, it's more about creating a system and then using habits to enforce the behavior.

This can help you stay ahead where most salespeople fall short. A good goal to strive for is staying one step ahead of your manager. Make hygiene a nonissue. When your pipeline is spotless, you can better focus on closing deals. Have crystal-clear next steps written in your notes. A habit I would always recommend is setting time to do admin after a call so that you take care of it bit by bit and it doesn't pile up. Others block time at the end of the day.

Along with hygiene comes following up. I am a proponent of inbox zero, an organizational approach that keeps your inbox empty, because you don't let emails fall through the cracks. It's also important to actively stay on top of follow-ups in your tasks and calendar. Follow up and follow through. Following through is doing what you said you were going to do. The little things, done correctly, make a huge difference in sales. The more pride and precision you take with even the most boring details, the more you stand out, and the better you perform. Following up means not letting opportunity fall through the cracks because of your own inaction.

SYSTEM #4—PERFECT PRACTICE, NOT JUST PRACTICE, MAKES PERFECT

So many middle-performing salespeople I speak with practice on their prospects. They see sheer repetition alone as the way that they can get better. They rarely seek out feedback. They don't roleplay or listen to calls outside of the bare minimum, and their results show it. Perfect practice requires doing it enough where you don't just get it close to right, but you can do it in your sleep. Then you become the person that everyone comes to for questions—you become the star of your team.

SYSTEM #5—PIPELINE COVERAGE

Pipeline coverage is the ratio of your pipeline value to your revenue goal. So, if your pipeline is $1 million and your target is $250,000, you have four times the pipeline coverage ratio. So you would need a conversion rate of 25 percent to get to your goal.

It's also worth considering the sales revenue formula here. With the formula you can calculate best- and worst-case scenarios in reaching your goals. When people say, "You can't outsell math," this is what they mean.

Revenue = Opportunities × Close Rate × Price (or average contract value)

So, if you have twenty opportunities booked and your close rate is 20 percent and the average deal size is $10,000, then what is your revenue?

$$20 \times 0.2 \times \$10{,}000 = \$40{,}000$$

Said differently, if your average conversion rate is 20 percent and you have twenty opportunities, with a $10,000 deal size, you should be able to convert four deals to revenue, which would be worth roughly $40,000.

This is incredibly helpful for coming up with best- and worst-case scenarios. What if your close rate dips? What if you raise it by 5 percent? What if you get more out of your deals up front? Small changes have big results in sales, and this formula helps point that out concretely.

Which brings me to our next topic as it pertains to pipeline. Everyone who manages a pipeline in sales is subject to what is commonly called the *law of replacement*. This means that if you close (whether you won or lost) an opportunity, it needs to be replaced. This dynamic is true in every type of sales role. A common reason for huge peaks and troughs in performance is that a salesperson will be overflowing with meetings one month, and consequently not have much for the next. So, the month they're currently in will be solid, but with no pipeline to replace what they are closing, they set themselves up for a lackluster following month. Mastering pipeline coverage will get salespeople more sustainable results and help prevent the burnout associated with constant up-and-down performance.

RELEVANCE AND CUSTOMIZATION

The biggest way to not sound canned is to deliver relevant messages at the right time to specific people. Contextual selling. This is not loading up a cadence with a thousand contacts and sending them the same message. Rather, it emphasizes a highly targeted approach to interacting with your buyers. Here are the two best ways to do this:

1. Look out for triggers.
2. Probe for problems.

There's a third as well that we will cover next chapter, which is to segment prospects by group.

Earlier, we went over how the structured call was created by the industry to get salespeople to control the buyer. Selling in the modern world, in the age of the buyer, means ditching a long-drawn-out sales presentation centered on us for more of a conversation with our buyer. It means tooling our teams with many possible medications for their buyer's problems. There's no one way to treat patients, and there's no one way to build wealth. Likewise, there's no one way to sell.

Conversational sales is about training not just on presentation skills (although these are hugely valuable), but also on picking up on clues and cues. It's training salespeople how to have authentic conversations with other people that are squarely focused on helping them solve problems. It's not a relationship-based approached to sales, but it's not a challenger approach either. Conversational selling is about two people or groups of people coming together via dialogue to solve a problem, improve, or even gain enjoyment from your product. It doesn't end when the deal is closed because that's when the relationship is just beginning. It's a never-ending process of problem-solving for our prospects and customers via direct and indirect dialogue.

Favoring a conversational model on sales calls does not mean no structure. It means lightening up the structure. Smoothing out the rigid lines and formal nature a bit. Providing space for the buyer. Asking questions to reveal what's really going on. It's about leading with the problem and not the product. It's about giving your buyers space to breathe. It's about showing what you do, not telling.

One of my favorite ways to show what I do is via email. Email is still one of the most effective ways to earn a sale. But many sellers are dampening the effect of sales emails to generate interest and revenues for their brands because they send out the same canned messages to everyone. Creativity is lost, and they become automated email senders instead of salespeople.

Instead, you might use creative strategies to drum up interest in your brand via email. A few tips on email:

- Give yourself two minutes to find two pieces of information about your prospect.
- As a rule of thumb, try to stay away from attachments and silly GIFs. If you use a GIF, have it include your product so they can see, feel, and experience it.

🍀 Use video platforms to send custom videos via email.

🍀 Make the subject line look like an email you would send to someone you know.

🍀 Pay attention to the first sentence, because that's what buyers can see before they even open the email.

🍀 Use social media to help you stand out in email.

With phone calls, the sales industry has seen a downward trend of connect rates, the percentage of calls where someone picks up. I recommend using tools to automate the calling process by getting buyers on the phone using technology. Buyer defensive technology has increased, so this is a great way to keep up with that change. If you need help finding tools, feel free to email me at michael@callypso.io and I will be more than happy to give recommendations.

The reason tools that help connect you via phone with live buyers are so powerful is that they save you dialing time and ensure you get connected. Many salespeople I speak with consider calling and getting no answer to be the worst part of sales. These tools help alleviate this problem.

Once you're connected, it's critical that you embody the concept of pattern breaking in your calls. Pattern breaking just means doing the opposite of what people expect you to do, in a thoughtful way. The best place for this is the top of the call. How can you pattern break to not sound like a typical salesperson and instead stand out and start the relationship on the right foot?

Let's go over a few intros you can use to your cold calls:

> "Hey Tessa, this is Michael. I am calling over from Callypso. This is a sales call. Open to giving me a shot, and if it's not a fit we can go our separate ways?"

"Hey Sarah, my name is Michael. I am calling over from a company called Callypso.
Checking in to share a couple of pieces of
information on expansion sales and account
management. Would you be open to hearing
me out?"

"Hey Jane, I spoke with one of your team members, Sally. She said you were the best person
to speak with. I am calling from a company
called Callypso. Any chance now is a good
time to chat for a few minutes? I will be brief."

The use of pattern breaks typically come in once they have
a chance to respond and are trying to get off the phone. Instead
of going against the grain here, go with it.

"I'm running into a meeting; can you call me
back later?"

"I'm happy to give you a call back later. In order
to possibly save us time there, would it be OK
if I asked a couple quick questions to see if this
even makes sense?"

"Sure."

Now I have started a conversation and even gotten their
permission without being pushy.

What are some other ways you can think of standing
out while also not being pushy and considering the sales
experience?

If a buyer asks you if this is a sales call, just own up to it.
They are probably used to most people squirming their way

around the answer rather than providing a simple, confident, and direct yes. Don't start off the relationship on the wrong foot by fudging the truth right off the bat. Going back to the concept of confidence versus desperation, owning up to working in sales and even being proud of it is critical to success. Nothing alienates buyers more than dishonesty or even blurring the lines. I also think it's ironic when sales leaders themselves get frustrated when people try to sell to them. What do they tell their team to do all day if it's not to reach out to people?

While we're on the topic of calling, I am always surprised by the lack of voicemails people leave. You don't leave a voicemail expecting a call back or a sale (although it's great when that does happen). You leave one to stand out.

A couple of different tactics you can use here:

1. Point out that you've reached out on another channel:

    "Hey Kat, I just sent you an email showing the first part of how Callypso works. It seems like the part on task automation might be most useful, given my conversation with the account managers on your team. No need to call me back, but maybe you could offer your thoughts on that specific part? This is Michael with Callypso."

2. You can even use humor:

    "I know no one uses voicemail anymore, but I knew you wouldn't have this number, so I decided to leave one so you'd know I'm not some robot calling you about updating your car warranty. Giving you a ring from Callypso. Callypso is specifically for account managers and account-management leaders to help them get more expansion revenue and assist with net revenue retention. If that resonates at all, our website is callypso.co."

3. Try the customized approach:

    "Hey Sarah, I know that market research companies have been negatively impacted by the macroeconomy. I'm hearing that expansion sales can be harder these days, and deals that were once deemed safe are now facing some headwinds. Not sure what your experience has been like, but judging from your recent social activity it might be worth trading information. This is Michael over at Callypso."

Voicemail is a massively underutilized channel because people don't see it as having an immediate reward. Ironically, our inclination toward instant gratification keeps us from getting what we want—engagement from the buyer. But if we use voicemail as a tool to not get the sale but instead help the buyer remember who we are, then we will be much more successful in the other touches we make. I highly recommend using a customized, well-researched approach here. If the buyer feels like you understand them or have even done research on them, you are way more likely to get a reply. If they think you sent the same message to many people, you won't.

There are all sorts of ways to remain top of mind without coming across as sales-y or self-serving. Buyers often appreciate when you follow up with them because of how busy they are. You can use voicemails, small gifts, cards, messages, or other means. I have a friend who is in real estate. She leaves little bags of popcorn on potential clients' doorsteps that say "Just poppin' by" and gets great feedback and results from them. She also brings pie to people's homes around the holidays. She is a master of staying top of mind, and when they are ready to sell their homes, she's the one they call.

KEEP THINGS LIGHT

One way to cultivate a casual and conversational sales experience is through phrases and questions. Here are some common phrases that remove pressure from your buyer and help you be more palatable in a sales cycle, especially at the earlier stages of an engagement:

> "Maybe I am not reading the room correctly, but . . ."

> "No need to take any action here . . ."

> "Any chance you could . . . ?"

> "What would it look like if . . . ?"

Many people can remove this pressure, but they usually do it through deception:

> "I'm not trying to sell you anything."

> "How have you been?"

> "I'm offering a free demo."

The main goal here is to be thoughtful and empathetic. Prospects love questions that make them think, so long as you never come across as feeling superior. Similarly, you want to eliminate any and all "gotcha" moments in the sales cycle. For example, you want to avoid questions like this:

"Do you ever have problems with recruiting?"

Who doesn't? When the prospect invariably says that they do have issues, then the gotcha moment comes:

"Well, at ACME, we specialize in . . ."

The veil is torn, and they literally stop listening. What would be better here is avoiding the gotcha moment by allowing space for the prospect to voice their problems. What you really want is to show trustworthiness. People share valuable information with people they deem trustworthy. That information is what helps you close deals. To share information, they have to become vulnerable, and so when we jump too quickly because we're overly incentivized by the end result, we miss all that good stuff in the middle that will actually motivate them to take action. Trust creates an environment for vulnerability, and vulnerability leads to vital information you need for the sale to progress.

Here are three things I keep in mind before entering a call like this one:

1. **Show your research**—Share first.
2. **Share your understanding**—Get to the heart of their concern.
3. **Listen**—Create a safe space.

After your introductions on this call, you might say,

"Thanks, everyone, for being here today. I'm super excited to dive in and learn more about

you all and how we might be able to poten-
tially help. I know you all are here to talk about
recruiting, so I thought I would open the floor
up to you to help me understand what are the
pressing items that are top of mind for you
currently.

"I've done a little bit of research previously
and learned that you all have recently launched
a new initiative to meet your aggressive hiring
quotas for the year. Perhaps we could start
here and work from there?"

Another phrase to get people talking is "I'll pass the mic
. . ." Passing the mic creates a strong visualization that the
prospect has to talk. And talk a lot. When someone has a mic,
it's not for a few moments. It implies depth.

Prospects typically get excited when someone nails what
they're going through because so few people take the time to
feel what is hurting them. It's amazing how far you'll go just by
understanding them.

Other phrases to avoid:

"Again . . ."

"Like I said previously . . ."

"That's not how our business works . . ."

"To be honest . . ."

"No pressure, I don't want to talk badly about
the competition, but . . ."

"I'm not trying to sell you anything . . ."

"How have you been?"

"Does that make sense?"

The phrases I've shared so far that should be embraced or avoided are wildly different in how they come across to the buyer. The first is empathetic and leads with curiosity and eliminates assumptions. The second either implies the opposite of what the word or phrase means, is misleading, or applies pressure to the prospect, none of which is healthy to a buying cycle.

There's an additional debate about the use of yes/no questions in sales. I think questions should be open ended and breathe oxygen into sales calls by allowing the prospect plenty of space to say what they think out loud, but there is also room for yes/no questions in the sales process. Time on this debate could be better spent focusing on whether the question serves the purpose of furthering the sale rather than trying to prescribe rigid rules for salespeople. Imagine five really good open-ended questions followed up by a yes/no question that allows you to pivot to a new area or line of questioning. Seems valuable here. I'd stay away from hard-and-fast rules (we all have them), which are really just people's preferences. Hard to prove the efficacy of a preference. This is why I prefer testing and data over gut instincts. Getting granular about how to measure what is said is crucial.

Here are other useful questions to ask in sales:

"What about . . . ?"

"What would you do in this scenario?"

"Can you walk me through . . . ?"

"How might it look if . . . ?"

"Would you even want to . . . ?"

"Can you paint a picture for me . . . ?"

"Why wouldn't you just . . . ?"

"What are your thoughts on . . . ?"

"Let's pretend . . ."

"Here's what I thought about x; is that how you read it too?"

"How do you think about . . . ?"

"What would happen if . . . ?"

I also like to put an asterisk by questions when they ask them. When a potential buyer asks a question, it usually means there is a deeper question or concern underneath what they are saying. A light clarification on this can be extremely useful.

Let's use a simple example:

> Prospect: "Do you integrate with
> Microsoft 365?"
>
> You: "No."

Instead of emphasizing the negative and leaving it there, you could turn the question back around and see if it's really a problem:

Prospect: "Do you integrate with
Microsoft 365?"

You: "We don't. Is that a roadblock for you?"

Prospect: "Not necessarily. It would just really
help me internally to make the case if I knew
you integrated with our email client."

Let's do another.

Prospect: "Do you have the ability to build
custom dashboards?"

You: "Yes."

Don't stop there! Lightly see what the motivation is behind
the ask.

Prospect: "Do you have the ability to build
custom dashboards?"

You: "We do. Were you looking to build custom dashboards?"

Keep it simple. Not sales-y. Uncover what they care about
and the why behind the question without asking why.

Putting valuable systems in place, learning how to be dynamic for buyers, and being responsive moment by moment
are perhaps some of the most important sales lessons I have
learned. These have served as the foundational elements that,
once put in place, can ultimately be the deciding factor in having a fruitful or flatlined sales career. In order to excel at sales,
we must first master the systems that map to success.

In order to excel at sales, we must first master the systems that map to success.

TRY THIS

- Be a student of sales by learning many tactics, approaches, and methodologies.
- Once you become well versed in a few different methodologies, focus on situational awareness and how to apply the right message for the moment.
- Learn and borrow from other disciplines. Books, podcasts, and other material can be hugely valuable to sales.
- Consume the content your buyers are consuming to help you with your sales efforts. Understanding their landscape is just as critical as building your sales skills.
- The little stuff matters. Stay on top of the small habits, like data and the admin parts of the job, so you can stay focused on the big picture of closing deals.
- Find an accountability partner in sales, whether in person or virtual, whom you can bounce ideas off and stay motivated with.
- Block your calendar so that you can be productive. Never get to the end of a day and ask, "What did I do today?"
- Focus on building a system that works for you so when you walk away and come back to work, the system is there and you can rely on it to produce results. This helps with peace of mind as well as performance.

—

CHAPTER 5

LESS IS MORE

HOW TO BECOME BOTH EFFICIENT AND EFFECTIVE AT SALES

Early on in my sales career, I made a ton of cold calls. Some days I made thirty calls. Other days I made more than 150. The thinking was to book at least five meetings every day—no matter how many calls it took. And then when I actually did book those five meetings in a day, I still had this sinking feeling that it was not enough. My colleagues at that company all felt the same, and to date I have never seen people burn out so quickly.

I still see organizations that run their sales team like this. They focus on the "what" and not the "how," and their salespeople burn out quickly. Why do we always assume a lack of results is because of a lack of effort?

The how part of sales encompasses the total required parts to excel at sales added together. This includes activity metrics—like the number of emails sent and the number of calls made—but not *only* activity metrics. More specifically, it is the messaging, the positioning, the discovery, the sales experience, the intonation in your voice, the bounce back after setbacks, the learning to read people, the timing, the research, the customization, the strategy, and more. These are the leading indicators of success. The problem with the management style of my managers back in the day is they just focused on the what, the lagging indicators like the number of sales calls. You can make 150 calls. But what if they are all low quality? What if your messaging is off? What if you have bad data? What if you're targeting incorrectly? When I mastered the how, I was able to consistently do less but achieve more, and it was one of the most transformative lessons of my career. Getting it right is more important than getting more done.

It sounds counterintuitive, but it makes sense when you really think about it. Activity metrics are just one form of effort, but they are not the only form. We tend to want to say that if revenue is low, then it must be an effort issue and therefore an activity issue. I have managed hundreds of salespeople in my career; low results are almost never because of lack of effort. They've usually been because of lack of know-how.

If a salesperson's revenue is suffering, there are often much deeper issues than how many dials or emails they sent. Another major problem on the sales floor is that technology has given us the tools to reach our buyers faster than ever, but because we have lost a customized approach in favor of a one-size-fits-all strategy, we have desensitized our buyers in the process. Our one-size-fits-all approach isn't just with our methodologies, as in the previous chapter, but it's also in how we are reaching out on a very tactical level. The result is that buyers feel overwhelmed by the sheer volume of outreach, and they feel that very few of the messages they receive will help them reach their specific goals.

We do not invest nearly enough time and effort in coaching salespeople. It is so much easier to simply say, "Do more," than it is to come up with a proper diagnosis of what is not

Getting it right is more important than getting more done.

working and actually help them do it. A friend once told me that a VP at his company told him, "The best salespeople just figure it out." I find "advice" like this infuriating and counterproductive. The result of these combined problems is that we are making an already hard job incredibly harder, and it doesn't have to be that way.

But salespeople aren't off the hook either. Our quotas don't change just because we have a bad manager. We shouldn't stop taking responsibility for our professional growth just because the company we're working at currently might not have the right resources in place. To get better at sales and build a sustainable career, we have to take the reins ourselves. The top performers always do.

Let's talk about the what and the how parts of selling to swing the pendulum in a more sustainable direction for our sales teams. By focusing on quality over quantity, we can create a better sales experience for both buyers and sellers—and truly drive more revenue.

QUALITY TARGETING

Sarah is one of the top-performing salespeople I know. Before she was responsible for closing deals herself, her main job was to create opportunities, or qualified meetings for other people while she was learning the ropes. Every month the meetings that she generated converted to revenue at much higher rates than did those of other members of her team. The secret to her success was in the time she spent targeting the right people at the right accounts and then focusing on qualifying them properly.

First, she would come up with a hypothesis for what would make someone purchase her product. Instead of sending random messages to random people, she spent time figuring out if people matched her ideal customer profile (ICP), and then she didn't deviate from that in acts of desperation. She zoned in on the kinds of businesses that were more likely to do business with her company and got good at focusing only on them.

When I was working for an early-stage startup, we often referred to this dynamic as coming up with *microtheories*. A microtheory is basically a little hypothesis for why you should reach out to your buyer—a buyer-centered hypothesis. Most salespeople think, *I need to reach out to someone in order to hit my quota.* That is a "me-centered" reason for contacting someone. Other reasons we use to reach out can be weak because they don't allow us to stand out. Take, for example, reaching out to someone because they recently closed a round of funding. Companies are so used to being reached out to after a fundraising round with similar messaging types that it becomes easy to drown out the prospecting noise. So what if they closed a round? How can you solve a problem for them? Just closing a round by itself isn't a reason to reach out. You must connect the dots.

Let's take a different example. If someone has been hiring rapidly, maybe a seller could build a message around specific problems seen with that. Or maybe they've noticed a website optimization they might be able to help with and could point that out lightly. Maybe they know someone at the company. Maybe they could use technographic or firmographic information to create something specific for the prospect based on problems they commonly saw with that type of company or role. At Chili Piper, we found problems that companies typically faced as a persona (another way of saying job title) and highlighted those. The main point is our reason for reaching out has something to do with them and almost nothing to do with us.

The biggest success we had was with *triggers*. A trigger is a prompt for you to reach out to a prospect or customer based on some action they took or an event that occurred. For example, for postsales account managers, maybe there is an overage that prompts you to try to upsell more licenses. Ideally you would want to reach out well before that overage trigger. Maybe it's just a trend in that direction that prompts a conversation. Maybe a trigger is they're hiring. A trigger is a reason for you to reach out that is about them, not about you. How you craft the messaging around such triggers should be on how and why it solves problems, makes them better, saves them money, or helps them reach aspirational goals. This is not about how awesome your product is.

The next thing Sarah did was focus on the right people. She didn't waste time with people she knew had zero chance, or even just a smaller chance, of doing business with her. She knew her worth and focused her attention only where it mattered. She would do what we call *multithreading*, or prospecting on multiple people at a time at a company, where applicable, instead of just one person. She would send different messages to them and not the same canned message. Buyers make purchases in teams, and so from the very beginning she was incorporating this into her strategy. Sarah is going places.

The last thing she did was focus on qualification. First, she researched the accounts to make sure they were high quality and likely to convert to sales. She did not view setting meetings as an end. She viewed generating revenue as the end goal. Second, she was not afraid to disqualify accounts, maybe even ruthlessly. This focus on quality of conversion through identifying companies that best matched the ICP with the right people, at the right time, with the right context enabled her to excel. This helped her build trust with teammates as well. People who received meetings booked by Sarah knew they were high quality, which created a self-fulfilling prophecy that fueled her status in the company and results further.

Qualifying, for her, did not mean the archaic strategies

like BANT, an overly rigid qualifying system that uses an invasive questioning system with buyers without providing any value to them in return. The B stands for *budget*—does this person/company have a budget? The A stands for *authority*—does this person have the authority or even access to authority? The N stands for *need*—basically, does the prospect need your product? The T stands for the *timeline* the buyer has identified to make this happen. All this information is completely self-serving and offers little help to the buyer. So, what Sarah might do differently from the BANT method is ask questions that reveal problems and then give a tiny glimpse of how she might be able to solve them. As a buyer myself, I can tell you if I want your product bad enough and don't have a budget already established, I will go and find it.

Only after she found a problem, she would ask questions to legitimately determine if they could do business together—if their tech tools were compatible, for instance. Every company should define qualification differently because our customers are all different. These data points should be documented and irrefutable so that any salespeople would get the same result after having spoken to the prospect.

When it was Sarah's turn to get promoted into a more direct selling role, she understood how opportunities connected with revenue. Today she is the top performer on her new team and exceeded her quarterly quota well before the halfway mark of the quarter. She still prospects for herself today even though she technically doesn't have to—she wants to make money and do well in her role. She knows she can't just rely on other people to determine how much money she will make, and she can make more money by having a pipeline from varied sources. Sarah is the type of seller any company would stop in their tracks to hire immediately.

QUALITY MESSAGING

Of all the areas we can focus on to be more efficient, quality of messaging is often the most neglected by sales leaders. Quality of messaging refers to all correspondence we have with buyers—written, verbal, and visual. This includes social media messages, video, email, phone calls, voicemails, and more. When a salesperson is struggling with performance, this is the first area where I look. When people's sales are "sick" and in need of remediation, reviewing the messaging is usually the most revealing. You can prevent getting sick by taking your vitamins, which in the sales sense means listening to and reviewing your messaging regularly. This is often the single biggest tweak you can make to get the fastest improvement: regularly review your sales calls, emails, and messaging with teammates and managers to get feedback. It's usually the thing people want to do the least, but it has the greatest payoff in terms of helping performance.

Messaging is usually the area that takes the most work to improve. It takes practice. I typically recommend hyperspecific roleplays here. So frequently, we practice on our buyers. When I was just starting out, I would be amazed by all the senior salespeople that never practiced outside their live calls with customers. We normalize practice in all crafts, but when it comes to business, we wing it.

At one startup I visited, the sellers' prospecting emails read like the technical manual for a vacuum cleaner. They were literally emailing their customers the technical specifications of their product. This is more common among startups founded by product-oriented leaders. The first step was changing the messaging, and the second was shortening the messaging. The third step was showing what the product did visually. Not over the top, but one or two things that stood out to customers. We had data from customer interviews that told us why they bought and which features were most interesting. We then took the exact verbiage from our existing customers and incorporated it into our messaging for potential buyers. It worked like a charm and helped us speed up our rate of scale.

A common area where messaging is overlooked is in email replies from prospects. Most of the mass email tools don't look at positive or negative replies. They just look at replies as one big bucket. To tell the positive reply rate, for example, you usually must go in and manually check and calculate this number. What's often missed is how to craft messaging to those that replied but the answer was neutral or negative. Minor improvements in this area can help with optimizing across your entire pipeline.

Let's say the email says something like "Not interested." When faced with this simple response, many sellers give up and don't reply. You don't have to turn this into a sale to have an impact, but maybe your goal is to get this prospect to consider you in the future. Maybe the goal is to leave the door open. Maybe it's a follow-up in a week. You never know if you don't try. Maybe "Not interested" really meant something else, like "I have a deadline tomorrow and can't deal with this right now."

Back to our example:

> Danielle,
>
> Thanks so much for replying to my initial email—I really appreciate it. When people say they are not interested, it's usually one of two things. Either what I said in the previous email just didn't resonate, or today is not a great day.
>
> Any chance you fit into one of these buckets?
>
> If it's the former, I'll be happy to not reach

out again. If my timing is off, I hope we can keep the door open.

Thanks again for the quick reply.

Best,

Michael

I have never seen a sales leader coach about email replies. The focus is always on the original output: cold calls, demo calls, discovery calls, and outbound emails. These are all critical parts of the selling process, but the lack of focus on email replies shows a general neglect toward the concept of efficiency. If you're missing this, what other areas of optimization throughout your interactions with buyers are you missing? Focus on small optimizations across the funnel, and they will add up to be monumental in aggregate.

There are absolute gems in email replies, though, and people who reply are often easier to talk to because they already *replied* to you. Most of the time if you are getting noes, objections, or lukewarm responses via email, you can turn those around by being radically buyer-centric. Sometimes this reveals that you're having a problem with targeting, like those described in the previous section. Attention to the smaller details is revelatory of the larger picture. Another tip to help with efficiency here is to call people that have opened the email but didn't reply.

While we are on the topic of people who have interacted with you, one of my favorite places to prospect is with closed lost opportunities. With closed lost opportunities, prospects have in some capacity engaged with your sales team before. They know the drill. The key for me has always been to simply figure out why they didn't move forward. Look for clues in the notes. Check the account history. Was it a product feature that you didn't have but now do? Was the timing just not right? Did the original prospect leave the company? There are all sorts of clues and minor tweaks you can make to excel where others have failed. I've won countless deals just months after other salespeople closed lost opportunities. The biggest piece of advice here is to come up with a theory as to why they didn't buy before, then think about how you might change that narrative. If it was a product feature, maybe you have released that. If it was timing, maybe you will spend extra time on discovery there to see why. Then maybe you can unearth problems that you might be able to help with in this moment.

Customized messages to prospects can also prevent you from being labeled as spam. The less you're labeled spam, the less your email goes to the spam folder. The less you go to the spam folder, the more you're delivered to people's inboxes, and the chances of them opening your email increases. What would you do if suddenly your mass email tools were taken away and you had to email everyone individually? We led a peer-to-peer training on email deliverability and how to customize emails regularly to stay ahead here. If your company hasn't done this, volunteer to lead it.

This prompts the question, What is the role of mass-emailing in this new world of selling? Do we abandon tools that enable this? Do we customize everything? The problems that we face as sellers considering this change in the world of buying are very real and impact the industry in substantial ways. It's my personal belief that those mass-blasting buyers to no avail are going to be the ones missing goals, losing money, and not carving out a successful sales career for themselves. I can teach just about anyone to load up and send out prewritten emails to groups of people. Where's the sales in that? The future of sales looks more like the future of other well-worn industries, where you really must be a student of the craft to excel. I believe this is a good thing.

Activity without efficiency is just noise. And noise makes it harder for everyone, not just you, to get their points across to the buyer. Noise is where we are today. Efficiency is where we want to be.

QUALITY ACTIVITY

Activity is the one area we hear the most about from our managers. What we don't hear is that we can improve this by focusing on ratios, not just numbers. We can use technology to help with our connect rates, and therefore our overall activity can go down while our overall results can go up. On a personal level, the months where I made the most phone calls were not my best-selling months. Activity is not equated with success. The strongest managers show salespeople how to get the most out of the deals they are working.

Sending more customized messages will help improve the open and reply rates to our emails, again resulting in a less-is-more dynamic. Fewer emails sent, but we get more back from them. The more we focus on quality, the less activity we must do. But no matter how good our quality piece is, we must engage in some level of activity to reach our goals. We tend to remember that less is more only during economic downturns. But what would it look like if we always worked that way?

One way to do this is to work backward from your goal. If you need twenty meetings booked in one month and the average number of calls per meeting is thirty, and there are twenty business days in the month, then you must make six hundred calls to get to your goal. This ends up being thirty calls a day to reach the bare minimum goal. This is a rough number to illustrate the concept, but you can work backward with email, calls, or both. Then if you are above or below your goal, you can gauge your efficiency relative to the average your company usually sees.

I prefer to think of activity like compound interest and consistency. Quality of activity is more about having a system in place than anything else. It's about having good sales habits that you are committed to every day.

Activity without efficiency is just noise. And noise makes

it harder for everyone, not just you, to get their points across to the buyer. Noise is where we are today. Efficiency is where we want to be.

QUALITY TIMING

Recently a mentor of mine told me a story about one of his clients. They were working an enterprise deal, and out of the blue the company stopped responding. The client got upset about this and shared his thoughts with my mentor. Then several months later, the enterprise company replied out of the blue, ready to move forward.

What my mentor's client realized and learned from asking questions was that he mistook radio silence for disinterest. Many things happened on the buying side that he never even realized. First, the customer had a huge technical release that diverted all resources. Month one disappeared. Then the company started prepping for an initial public offering (IPO). Budgets were frozen for months.

About five months later the economy shifted, and they decided not to try to IPO. The company then reached back out to my mentor's client because the timing was right for them.

So much can happen that we don't see. Instead of responding with pressure in trying to get the sale, trying to understand just a little bit of our prospect's world can reveal so much of what we need to do. Pressure is not going to work on a large potential enterprise customer who is having an extremely chaotic behind-the-scenes drama unfold. Understanding is your biggest friend in sales. Never shoot in the dark.

Let's take another example.

Recently I was trying to fundraise for my startup, and an investor (let's call them "investor A") was moving at a very slow pace. I had given investor A a head start over other investors I was speaking to because I'd known them longer. The demeanor of investor A was as if they had already won the deal (another sales lesson here—the deal is never won until the money is in the bank and the dotted lines are signed). They had many complicated steps and were moving much slower than the other investors. They also made strange comments in the discovery phase that were off-putting to me and my cofounder. But what they didn't realize was that I felt pressured to get a deal done because my lawyers put a time limit on closing the deal. My legal team was trying to protect me, so they put a deadline in the terms of agreement. We had thirty days to close a seven-figure deal.

One day my lead investor set up a call with a group of investors, let's call them "investor B." The call with investor B was completely different from the one with investor A. They were engaged, offering new perspectives on the market I hadn't thought of, and the biggest thing for me was they moved fast. They understood that if we didn't, they were going to miss out, because they had missed out before. So, they called me right after my pitch to them and gave me an offer. I took the offer, and later that afternoon I received another offer, completing the fundraising round and denying investor A a seat at the table. That was one of the most painful rejections I have ever had to deliver.

In this example, I was evaluating the investors just as much as they were me, but investor A acted like we had all the time in the world. Had they moved at a faster rate and showed me their interest rather than making me jump through complicated hoops, I would have been more inclined to do business with them.

It goes the other way too. If you're trying to close a deal and the buyer is giving every sign that they are not yet with you, hit the brakes. Pace really does influence deals. Make sure you're walking in lockstep, or you might add unnecessary risk to what should otherwise be a simple process. If investor A had simply realized how concerned I was about the thirty-day deadline, they would have understood that I was going to close a deal as fast as I could with the right type of firm. Having me wait around and not closing the deal was like putting a piece of steak in front of a dog and saying, "Don't eat it." They could have also asked me a few more questions around my timeline. They could have even said, "If you get another offer, will you call us to let us give an offer as well?" None of this happened.

This dynamic happens on all types of sales calls. Maybe the buyer just wants to buy and get on with it. Or conversely, maybe the buyer needs more time or something happens in the buyer's personal life. So many things can change how quickly the buyer responds. And many times, expectations on both sides are not spoken aloud or discovered until it is too late.

Watch for important cues and signals and respond accordingly. Ask about how soon they are willing to decide. Ask if they have any pressures or deadlines. One time, I was helping a salesperson on my team and learned that the buyer needed help getting approval from her new boss, but also had a major deadline. We got on a five-minute call with her, then scheduled a call with her boss. We worked backward from the deadline and got the deal done very quickly. When she had space to voice her concerns aloud, we addressed them head-on and gave her material to expedite the approval with her boss. Whenever you are experiencing friction via email with buyers, ask them for a five-minute call to go over the details. It's a low-pressure ask that allows you to hash out details without wasting time going back and forth over email. It's an especially great tool to use for deals that are on the fence or have hit a roadblock.

Buyers also often want to work with vendors who respond sooner and on their timeline. That's why it always baffles me when vendors have a Contact Us page on their website but it takes a long time to hear back from the sales team. Pace is an important determinant to success. In this buyer's world we live in, you'd better be the very first one that replies to people's sales inquiries.

QUALITY COLLABORATION

It's not just pace that matters in deal acceleration. When I was being trained in sales for the first time, our managers were almost militant about the need to speak with the decision maker (DM). If we passed pitches to "influencers" (i.e., someone who influences decisions but doesn't make them alone), it was frowned upon. The DM was put on this pedestal, like you must get to this mythical human to get the money that will set you free. The concept of selling to the DM for the sale I was doing did make sense at the time; however, there were countless examples of an influencer being the reason a deal closed.

But most sales are not that simple. Most companies have shifted from an environment where the DM made all the decisions to one where decisions are made as a team. And sure, not having an economic buyer with power who is sponsoring this deal is catastrophic, but in this modern world of selling, there are also other threats. Other people can block deals. Therefore, we need to replace the thinking of "Get to the DM" with building consensus so you don't get blocked by some unforeseen circumstance or person.

So, who are some of the people on the team? Besides the DM and the influencer, there is often an approver, someone who must do work to get your project implemented and thus can be a blocker. This could be someone in legal, finance, procurement, or IT. Or you could need to deal with an individual contributor in a customer-facing role. For example, if it's revenue operations, maybe they have access to the CRM and technology stack. If you're trying to sell them, you're creating work for them. They are often very protective of their environments and especially of security.

If one thing is clear about the way companies are buying today, it's that companies are more likely to buy in teams than ever before. Yet we still are using a sales process that doesn't sell to them as a team. For example, we have them talk to junior salespeople who ask basic questions. Then the next salesperson asks different variations of the same questions. By the time they become customers, that information is lost, and the account-management and customer-success teams re-ask these questions. How can we better sell in teams to meet buyers where they are?

For starters, as boring as it may be, note capturing is critical. Beyond just note-taking, though, teams responsible for selling should compile mutual action plans, notes, and account plans that can be transferred to teammates who inherit our deals as customers. This creates a seamless buyer experience. What were the customer objectives in buying the tool? Were those met? These are your gold mines for expansion. Sales is not just being good at getting the first deal. It's growing your current customer base for the lifetime that they are with you.

I'm not going to belabor this point, as we've covered it in a previous chapter, but do not let the buyer regurgitate information they've already said. Instead, always build on what was done previously. Teams can also do a better job of strategizing together. Selling in teams is one way to refresh the way we sell and provide a more equitable buying experience.

This moves us to the concept of champions. The champion is the person who can help you navigate the murky waters of how to get a deal done. They are your conduit into the buyer's company. They are the person or people fighting for you on the buyer's side. A good way to spot a champion is they do the work and are often the most enthusiastic about moving the deal forward. Don't just listen to what someone says to determine whether they are a champion; watch what they do. Recruiting them to be on your side is one of the most pivotal components to getting a deal across the board.

For our postsales teams, it is especially important to find multiple champions. The second the initial champion leaves the company, the deal could fall apart. Having more than one champion is an effective way to mitigate churn and increase sales. This is called *multithreading* your champion.

There are often individual contributors who must want to use your product: The manager must roll it out. Operations, legal, and procurement/finance usually have pronounced roles. There can be approvers or multiple department heads. And finally there's the person who signs on the dotted line. Thinking of the sale in terms of consensus as well as project management can help the seller build a coalition of support in the organizations they sell to and outline the microsteps along the way to get it done. In today's world of selling, you aren't just selling to your champion and the person who likes you the most at a company. You're selling to them, then to their team. You're selling to the individual contributors, then to the upper managers. After all that, many teams require procurement, operations, IT/security, and legal to approve deals. We are truly selling to an entire company more than we ever have before.

Many of the salespeople I have worked with over the years treat the process of understanding timelines and next steps after an initial call in an overly simplistic way. One thing that always helps me is to think of the little steps—the seemingly unimportant microtasks that need to be completed for a deal to close—then work with the buyer to achieve those milestones. Turn into a project manager, but don't be pushy and overbearing. Get on the same side as your champion, then work with them to peer behind the curtain into the company. Be balanced and respectful, but also read the room. Crafting mutual success plans can be a powerful tool for getting the desired result.

Perhaps one of the most important concepts when selling to teams is the idea of matching our buyers. If they sell in a team, we do too. If they deploy resources, we match them at every step. When they bring in a VP really early, I come to the table too. If they get technical on their side, we bring in our CTO. Maybe this dynamic is different depending on the size of your company, but using your resources and selling as a team is going to be critical to thriving moving forward. Don't sell in isolation. Ask for help. Demonstrate the ROI to your bosses. Having them directly supporting you can help you lock things down. Show them a report of leadership-assisted deals. People start moving when they see data. Data is your biggest and best friend when managing up within your own company, especially at the director level and above. Show this data, especially when it was a big deal or large revenue that was assisted. This doesn't mean they close the deal for you. It means they match the seniority that the buyer's side projects.

It goes without saying that your number one person in a buying process is your champion. They are the person you get on the same side with first in a buying cycle. They are the one that helps you get everything done and is your eyes and ears on the inside. But more than that, you need to be their champion too.

The other day I made a couple of mistakes. The first mistake is that I didn't prepare my champion when they went and made an ask inside a company. It was a simple ask, and they came back with all sorts of objections from the internal approving team. We agreed that the best next step would be a call with me and him directly.

Then I made another mistake. I didn't let my champion prepare me. I got on the call and was immediately caught off guard.

"So, what does your tool even do?"

The approver didn't even know what I was trying to sell. I really dropped the ball here.

The takeaway for me was to always prepare your champion. Even when you think they understand your product. Then you need to let them prepare you adequately as well. Don't show up to a call blindly. Make sure you have a plan and know what the goal is and what the outcomes should be.

What does the internal team need to see? What are they fearful of? Who are the blockers? Who are the allies? Build the case by building your own buying team and uncovering what concerns people have. Get out in front of them. Build consensus by matching their buying team with your own.

The best people to buy from you are the ones who already have bought from you. Yet we often focus on "net new" almost at the expense of revenue. Referrals, existing business, and our customers can all be forgotten. The companies and salespeople that outperform the rest don't regard sales as a singular exercise of closing a deal and treating that as the end. It's just getting started!

TIE IT ALL TOGETHER

One of the most important parts of tying these concepts together is creating a tiered system for all your clients and potential prospects. I recommend a simple three-tiered system. Tier 1 are your best targets. These are the companies that you dream of—the perfect matches and fits on both sides. Every message you send to them should be completely customized—not mass-blasting. Send them well-thought-out, well-researched, customized messages that are specifically tailored to them. These are the customers that you study, watch, engage with on social media, and learn from the most.

Tier 2 is also very good. They're the ones that are very high quality but maybe not the status of the dream accounts above. So with these you can send messages that might be somewhat customized, but not to the full 100 percent threshold.

Then you have your Tier 3s. For these, it is OK to use cadencing tools. That doesn't mean you aren't tailoring the cadence specifically to them, but you're also trying to get just a little bit of volume here. Maybe this is your emerging-markets target. Maybe it's a target that you can still sell to technically but might be harder for you. Maybe they have a slightly different technology stack or employee head count.

You can create a tiering system for your presales team and then a separate one for postsales. Presales tiering is based on your ICP. Postsales tiering is based on potential for growth.

The kicker here is that we, the sellers, love to treat everyone the same. In sales this might not be good for the customer. The needs of a fifty-person startup are very different from an enterprise company with five thousand people. Therefore, our approach should be different here. The level of research and customization should directly correspond to whether a company is Tier 1, 2, or 3.

Segment your accounts by defining Tiers 1, 2, and 3, then correspond your sales strategy to this segmentation.

TRY THIS

- Create a tiered system for your prospects and customers. This grouping will help you know the level of customization and strategy behind your approach.
- Relentlessly focus on qualification.
- Align yourself to revenue, not just meetings booked.
- Focus on the small areas for optimization up and down your pipeline. Small improvements result in big changes to your outcomes.
- Focus on targeting the right people in your ICP, and don't deviate from this focus.
- Double down on your attention to detail with messaging. Tailor your messaging to your prospect by helping them solve problems.
- Focus on collaborating internally at your company to sell as a tribe. Match power with power.
- Multithread your champions wherever possible.
- Timing is important. Radio silence for you can mean chaos for your buyer.

—

CHAPTER 6

CREDIBILITY AND VISIBILITY

HOW TO BE MEMORABLE IN A WORLD THAT CAN'T REMEMBER YOUR NAME

When an old friend's cat died, the Chewy.com team sent her a care package. She posted about it all over Facebook, proclaiming how thoughtful the team was. When it comes to brand loyalty and purchasing, where do you think she will spend her money on her pets for the rest of her life? Brands that engage us on a human level, especially outside the sales motion, are the ones that make a lasting impact in our minds. Are you helping me? Are you looking out for me? Or do you just care about earning that next commission check? I can't tell you how many times I hear questions like this from buyers.

Posts praising Chewy have been known to go viral not only because people like what they're doing but also because many people have had that same experience with the brand. They all then collectively amplify the brand because of a shared experience.

BRAND MATTERS

In the B2B world, this dynamic unfolds daily, and it has real re-percussions for the overall health of a business. Take Gong.io, for example. Their main rival is a tool called Chorus. Both are revenue intelligence platforms. When the CEO of Gong was asked by the CEO of a company where I used to work how he was going to beat a better-funded, better-known adversary, he purportedly said that they were going to execute better.

That they did. But a huge element to what set them apart in the mind of the market was their branding, notably among their sales team. What became obvious to me and the other evaluators on our team was that we wanted to go with Gong because they simply had a better brand. That brand gave them more credibility. So we didn't choose just because of the soft-ware and the sales experience. We chose because we felt the brand (a) was something we wanted to be associated with and (b) had greater competency as a company because of this in-tentional branding. The brand became an extension of the sales experience.

So what were some of the things they did?

First, they educated the market and made selling easier on the marketing side. They released interesting articles, blogs, and studies. They even launched a Super Bowl ad. This trick-led all the way down to the individual-seller level as well. They were guests on podcasts, wrote meaningful articles them-selves, contributed in a very public way. The brand was hav-ing fun because the individual people were having fun, and the material they produced was available to everyone, not just their sales targets. Gong remains a massive player in the space, where their number one competitor, Chorus, was forced to be acquired by a much larger company, ZoomInfo.

But it's not just that the strongest brands are getting their salespeople to post on LinkedIn. It's that the brands view their people as extensions of the brand and therefore encourage them to focus on reputation—industry reputation, personal reputation, and reputation as salespeople as well. They are focused on every possible interaction, no matter how large or small, as being a collective reflection of brand. We are all brand ambassadors. The lines between sales and marketing are more blurred than they have ever been—and that is arguably good for all of us. The entire company should align toward revenue growth, and therefore marketing and sales should work together as a team to drive this growth.

We're more likely to do business with people who engage with us in a way that leaves a positive impact when we aren't actively in market for a product as well. The buyer simply remembering your name or your company's name is an achievement in today's world—that's the *exposure piece*. Exposure is them seeing and remembering you. Gong championed this through their branding, not just from their marketing team but also from their employees and salespeople being extensions of that overall brand strategy.

They created minimarketers all focused on their own personal brands. *Personal branding*, then, was their intentional effort at influencing, informing, and educating others publicly.

Think of the million products out there in each category. It's overwhelming, even to people who study this stuff. Now think what happens if people are already familiar with and have a favorable opinion of your brand. Then when they are in market, boom. They are more likely to choose you.

I think the brands that do the best today and, in the future, will be those that double down on this and use creative branding to become memorable. At Chili Piper, we had our sales team send hot sauce to prospective customers. We amassed hundreds of thousands of views on social media from campaigns and creative fundraising announcements. Every time we did a creative campaign, our sales improved.

Or take Airbnb. They famously diverted resources away from traditional paid channels, time and again, to focus on brand marketing—and their results increased. Branding works because it is emotional, like humans are.

REPUTATION MATTERS MORE

Familiarity and exposure are key ingredients to being memorable. This is one big reason why every salesperson should 100 percent be investing in their brands. You build familiarity not only by reaching out when you want something in return, but by being genuinely helpful to your buyer and anyone who interacts with your brand—your brand being you.

And then whenever you do reach out, you make it about them and their problems. You step into the world of being a giver and not a taker. This is a big reason why promoting your own products almost never works as a content strategy by itself. The personal gain is very obvious, and it's hard for people to see what's in it for them.

But it's not just branding that counts. I recently brushed off an account executive who was prospecting me. I didn't need the product yet, and the timing was off. Then down the road, someone from another company in the space, a company I viewed favorably, recommended that original company. I thought back and remembered the initial salesperson was seemingly competent, thoughtful, and friendly. I went and purchased a couple of products from her. It's been about an eight-month relationship now, and I am very satisfied with my experience. So, it's not just brand that matters. I personally view it this way: *reputation is the umbrella under which brand falls*. Brand is an extension of reputation, and it is intentional. Are you the type of person that will get referrals from a multitude of sources?

To me, the difference between brand and reputation is credibility. Personal brand is more about exposure, and personal reputation is more about credibility. That is why I start with reputation first and then move toward personal brand. Personal brand without credibility ends up feeling a bit empty to our buyers. Reputation is how others view and perceive you—but this should not be a passive exercise.

Here are some key considerations when you're thinking about your personal reputation:

1. Always value honesty above all else.
2. Problem-solving for others should be at the top of your list.
3. People must believe right off the bat that you're in it for them.
4. Salespeople must provide a strong sales experience.
5. Intentionally work on what you are known for.
6. Professional competency is crucial.
7. Will people learn from you meaningfully?
8. Can people trust you?
9. Do you have deep domain and sales expertise?
10. Are you fun to work with?

These are some crucial questions I ask to practice reputation management as an active rather than passive exercise. When you're active about your reputation, it puts you in the driver's seat and accelerates your career in sales.

Personal brand, on the other hand, is a little bit different. The term is thought to have come from a 1997 article by Tom Peters entitled "The Brand Called You." Since then, it has taken on a life of its own, with thousands of conversations struck up online daily about the topic. Personal brand is not just what you post on LinkedIn or Twitter. It encompasses everything about your interactions, not just with buyers, but all the different ways in which you publish material for others' consumption. I think of branding as a "one to many" exercise, where you disseminate information to many people as one individual. Having a developed personal brand means pushing the odds of buyers doing business with you in your favor in a very intentional way. It can also accelerate your career by exposing you to people at companies where you might want to work one day.

PROBLEM BRANDING

But what if there was also a more meaningful way to engage with buyers? I think personal brand is crucial. I think it's great when people celebrate personal wins publicly and even focus on gaining maximum visibility for themselves. Expertise and credibility are also necessary elements to personal brand.

But what if we took it a step further? What if I mixed up the personal branding with what I refer to as *problem branding*? Problem branding is when you highlight the challenges, agitations, and frustrations of your buyer. You invite them to the conversation. You poke the bear. It's that devil in the way.

This type of branding pivots from the typically congratulatory comments to deeper and more thoughtful engagement. With so much of branding and social media coming across as transactional and even lacking substance, it's the people that make you think and go deeper who I believe will stand out and have better results in the long run. Be a news reporter, discovering problems and solutions for your buyer. In a world where everyone is trying to become an influencer and gain more

It's any interaction someone has with you. It's realizing that a no today isn't a no tomorrow so it's not worth burning a bridge, because sales cycles are short in comparison to people's memories of bad experiences.

followers, it's the people who genuinely end up helping others improve that will not only make a bigger impact but further their own brands as well.

There are so many posts that do well at the exposure aspect but can go a lot further on the *conversion piece*. The conversion piece for sellers can mean converting someone to become a customer, or even just converting them to engage more. Maybe they sign up for an email list and actively choose to engage with you further somehow. This "wanting to engage more" mindset is hugely critical.

Once you get someone to engage, how do you make it about them so that they want to engage more? This usually happens for a few reasons: they see you as an authority, they want to learn from you, they enjoy following your success, or you demonstrate you're having fun.

I believe most salespeople can go much further in creating their own personal brands, for sure. But I also believe that once we do the exercise of developing our brands, we can optimize by focusing on reputation and problem branding as well. There should not be gaps in who we are online and offline, and we should speak about areas in which we have genuine expertise. Branding without substance can leave a poor impression in people's minds. We talk about the positives of branding all the time, but what if exposure without substance causes people to not work with us?

DEVELOP A TRUSTWORTHY BRAND

Every salesperson on the planet should be interacting with their prospects and customers outside the regular sales motion. Ideally you should be interacting with people in your industry directly as well. Social media, events, podcasts, and webinars are just a few examples. You can even use material from your social engagement and incorporate it into your prospecting efforts. For example, if you see a prospect post on a certain topic, you can use that for customizing your messaging later.

Trustworthy branding is that transcendent place we all want to get to—where we are seen as a genuine authority, what we say is respected publicly in our space, and people view us as competent and honest. This is where expertise meets brand.

Part of being trustworthy is intimately knowing the landscape you are selling into. It's not enough to be good at sales. You must be good at the context in which you are selling. You should read what your prospects read. Participate in the groups they participate in. Build familiarity with buyers before they ever reach out to you. One of the best ways to build a trustworthy brand is to really know the lay of the land in which you are selling and also to be excellent at selling.

Building a trustworthy brand is not just posting a lot of content. It's how people think of you when you're not around. It's any interaction someone has with you. It's realizing that a no today isn't a no tomorrow so it's not worth burning a bridge, because sales cycles are short in comparison to people's memories of bad experiences. It's being authentic. It's the dynamite conversation you had. It's listening, really listening to what a buyer said and delivering to precisely what motivates them. It is the overall sales experience they have with you that makes them think and envision how the relationship would unfold if they were to become a customer.

When we transition from personal brand to trustworthy brand, we go from "Look at me" to

- More "This is what I learned"
- An offline experience that backs up our online presence
- More authenticity

- More helpfulness to others
- Being contributors to our community

I think people are fatigued with branding for branding's sake. The ones that stand out are congruent online and offline, and they have the street cred to back up what they're saying. There's a certain emptiness to being an influencer without meaning.

People make a company tick. The cumulative effort of everyone in a company is what drives sales forward. That is the brand. Your individual, personal brand contributes not only to your success but to the company's. This brand you can also take with you from company to company. No one owns this brand but you. So building your own trusted voice and brand, even if you have more learning to do (we all do), is crucial.

AVERSION VERSUS INTENTION

There's another point to being trustworthy that I see unfold quite a bit. Some salespeople may feel general *sales aversion*. Sales aversion is another way of saying reluctance. When you feel reluctant to do something, a common thing that happens is you become avoidant. When you become avoidant, you can often mask this reluctance through being busy in other areas. You spend thirty minutes researching an account instead of picking up the phone or sending an email that will actually engage the buyer. It also happens with branding. The point of being proactive with personal branding isn't to spend all our time on brand. It's to spend *some* time on brand so that it helps our outreach efforts and helps our buyers. The overwhelming majority of our time should still be on our regular job. Brand is not a distraction, it's an intention. It should be additive.

CRAFTING OUR BRAND

In crafting a brand, it's not enough for your audience to know you—until they know you can help them. Our own brands can be just as powerful as a company's brand, if not more, because at the end of the day people still buy from people.

Here are some questions to ask yourself to help develop problem-oriented content:

- What is an unconventional viewpoint I/we have that no one else has that can help people get better?
- What are the five biggest problems for our buyer, and how can I help illustrate solutions to those problems?
- How can we challenge people to view this problem differently in a way that helps them?

USE THEIR LANGUAGE

A big part to helping with the conversion piece is messaging. Messaging is the actual words we use to convey meaning in branding but also in sales. A frequent mistake I come across with this is using our *own* jargon, terms, and so on in messaging. Whether online or offline, using language in our buyer's terms is critical to success.

The other day I was walking around in New York City with my cofounder and one of his friends. We were starving and I really wanted pizza. I always want pizza. I looked up a pizza shop on Yelp, and we rushed to get there. We arrived at the parlor one minute past closing time. I opened the door and said, "I know you're closing, but any chance there's a way to squeeze us in?" They waved us off and continued laughing and talking to each other in Spanish. So, I did what any self-respecting sales-person would do. I switched languages, literally.

"Disculpa, lo siento, pero tenemos mucho hambre. ¿Puedo pagarte con efectivo si tienes algo de comer?" Translation: Excuse me. I'm sorry, but we're really hungry. I can pay you in cash if you have anything to eat?

"¿Cuanto tienes?" How much do you have?

The attendant walked to the large oven and said that someone had never picked up their order and it was going to be tossed. He grabbed a massive amount of food from on top of the oven and gave it to me. I gave him eighteen dollars for what was probably sixty-five dollars' worth of food that was going to be thrown away.

As crazy as it sounds, I see this happening all the time on sales calls we have at work: salespeople speaking different languages from their prospects. A prospect calls it a "PM," and you call it something else. Sellers try to get prospects to use their words and naming conventions instead of the other way around.

If you want to stand out in the buyer's mind, the first rule is to use their language, literally. If they call it a BDR (business development representative), you call it a BDR. If they call it something else, match them. Speaking their language is the most basic way to stand out in sales.

PERSONAL TOUCH AND CUSTOMIZED OUTREACH

Sometimes having a good reputation is being the best at running a sales call, getting amazing referrals, or being the very best at prospecting, whether it be cold-calling or emails. Reputation goes so much further than our online identities alone.

Over the years, I have also heard tremendous stories about

people sending personalized gifts to stand out. I always recommend doing this in an extremely individualized way so the buyer does not feel like you are trying to bribe them. The gift must make sense and resonate. Look for "wow!" moments and opportunities. Creativity should be the focus. With that creativity comes impact.

I've been sent all types of gifts that I have regifted to other people because they didn't make sense to me. I have enough company-branded socks and bookbags for a lifetime. Some of my favorite gifts were when someone had a specific reason for sending me something and it was unique to me or a certain situation. Maybe I mentioned I liked to cook, and they read that about me and sent me a cookbook. I've tried to do the same with my buyers. For example, I realized that a prospect needed to save time, so I bought them dinner one night to specifically give them time back in their day. That saved the deal. There are a few select companies that are excellent at a more personalized approach to gifting.

Make the gift contextual to the moment. Send them flowers on their birthday or a gift when a big life event happens. The entire point of treating sales as a craft is to loosen the rigid lines of sales so that our buyers feel more at ease. Customers don't want to feel like transactions. They want to feel more like we are on their side, not taking something from them. I feel like business has leaned in the transactional direction for a bit too long. The same way our prospecting methods need an update, so does our brand strategy. Imagine if all your competitors posted on blogs and socials, had podcasts, spoke at conferences, and so on. My bet is you would double down on quality and creativity. Any of the difficulties we are having in sales today might be a good thing. It forces us to up our game— almost a return to how people did business before computers existed. A return to the age when we worked with people we knew something about. People we trusted.

CRAFT YOUR OWN THESIS STATEMENT

When someone is trying to purposefully build their brand for the first time, they usually say something like, "I want to do it, but I just don't know how to get started." Other people simply get started, but their content doesn't always land because there is no clear, unified angle or message.

This is why I highly recommend starting with a thesis statement for personal branding. A thesis statement is a one- or two-sentence description of your unique abilities, knowledge, and skills combined that offers up some unique perspective to others.

Think about how influencers and even microinfluencers build a following. The most successful ones have carved out a niche. Even niches within niches. This is intentional. Some specialize in SEO marketing and seek to teach you about that very narrow area. Others are sales coaches, and so they post from every possible angle centered on helping people get better there. There are fintech influencers, and the list goes on and on.

What is your unique perspective that you are good at and passionate about? Then within that category, what is your given area of expertise that you can be trusted on?

Carving out a niche doesn't mean you don't ever post about things outside of that. When I got started, this was my thesis statement:

> *To be known for building and supporting sales teams through coaching, training, and enablement in the B2B SaaS sales community.*

My reasoning behind this thesis statement was I felt most sales teams weren't adequately trained or supported—something I am deeply passionate about fixing. The less selfless

126

reason was that I knew if I made my statement a little bit aspirational, it would help us with our recruiting and it would attract the type of candidates who wanted coaching.

I also made the statement specific. What is it? Coaching. Who is it for? Salespeople. Which ones? B2B SaaS. How good is it? Above the status quo.

It worked. In just a few months after I crafted my personal thesis, applications to sales roles *and* the company's revenues increased.

Once I had a thesis, the rest of my content was anchored to that, and it helped me come up with post ideas. The posts would come to me at all sorts of different times. I took the "write from the heart, edit with the mind" approach here. I would jot ideas down on my phone when they came to me on a run or in the shower or out with friends. I'd keep a list on my phone. Then back at my computer I'd edit them and make sure they were written in a way that was useful to others.

I had three very clear goals that were derived from this thesis statement:

- Goal #1—Recruit top sales talent.
- Goal #2—Solve problems for our customers.
- Goal #3—Build name recognition for a brand-new startup.

The thesis statement helped make these goals a reality.

Now that I have a company of my own, this thesis statement has changed completely.

My new thesis statement is this:

> *To be known for educating and inspiring B2B professionals and businesses on expansion sales, renewal management, account management, and the critical importance of net*

revenue retention for B2B companies across the globe.

I have a subthesis statement also, to *celebrate and pro-mote the success of our customers, employees, partners, and company.*

I want to do both the problem branding and the personal branding here.

MANAGING YOUR BRAND

Branding, for a seller, is when a buyer has an option to work with someone else or purchase in another way and they still choose you. Branding is our unfair advantage. Our buyers do have more options than ever before, so it's important to realize that when they are speaking with us, they are probably speaking to several other companies at the same time. When they speak with us, they are choosing to speak with us, and with that choice comes responsibility on our behalf to deliver exceptional experiences. We are also just one way they receive information, not the only way.

Being confident in sales is about recognizing the fact that the buyers have a choice in whom to work with, and it doesn't matter. Because you, the seller, are so easy to work with, you've built a great reputation, and you are memorable, they choose you. You are also unfazed by the fact that they are talking to others because you're confident first in your abilities and what you offer and then in how you and your product specifically solve the problem that they need help with in the moment. You go further than other salespeople.

Here are a few topics you can post on that aren't self-promoting or product promoting to help get you started:

- Express a unique angle on some common occurrence in the business world.
- Start a debate to get interesting answers on important questions from your network.
- Ask a thoughtful question with a bit of context for your network.
- Tell a compelling story with a key lesson or takeaway.
- Share a mistake you made.
- Post a short video or GIF describing how you solved a common problem your buyer faces.
- Say what everyone is thinking but no one else is saying.

TRY THIS

- Go above and beyond by remembering moments people might not otherwise expect you to remember, even special events in their lives. Send them something contextual to the moment. It can be small, like flowers or a card.
- Interact with your buyer's content and post content of your own. Create a running list on your phone of topics you'd want to talk about. Tracking engagement is a helpful way not only to improve but also to get over the initial fears you might have around posting content to social media.
- Create your own thesis statement. Map your content to this.
- Use their language. Pay close attention to how they use industry jargon, and mirror that.
- Focus on reputation first, brand second.

CHAPTER 7

THE EIGHT CARDINAL RULES OF SELLING

HOW TO LEVEL UP YOUR CRAFT WITH PROVEN LAWS FROM THE FIELD

Brett was never going to make it. The guy had a lot of experience, but it was clear that he was one of those people who essentially got to skip the regular hiring process because he knew someone who knew someone. It was like networking gone wrong, from my perspective. Nice guy. Terrible salesperson.

Brett had reached out with what felt more like a fact-finding mission than a curiosity to learn. I was in one department, he in another, so there was no real overlap between us. Someone recommended we connect to get to know each other, being that he was newer to the team. So we did.

In my first interaction with him, he said, "I'm excited to see how you all do things here. It seems like I have more experience than everyone, and I'm older too. But don't worry, seems like you have been here a while. Maybe you can listen to my calls every now and then. I once had a young person

The funny thing about sales is that it's a great equalizer.

like you listen to my calls, and some of the stuff he said was valuable."

I was dumbfounded. But he came with stellar references, so I decided to give him the benefit of the doubt. A few weeks later, I checked in to see how he was doing.

"Great," he said smiling. "Things are going really well. I've just had my first call and it went really well."

"First call"? That got me worried. By this time, there should have been revenue on the board and lots of calls in the books. This was a big red flag.

"Oh," I said. "That's great you had your first call. Though usually by this time people have had a few more at bats."

"Oh, I mean, I did have other calls. I just disqualified them all."

"Disqualified them all?"

"Yeah, they weren't ready to buy, so I just marked them DQ."

I was intrigued. There was simply no way that all the prospects he had were not interested. And even if they were, wasn't it his job to get them to buy? Out of pure curiosity, I went and listened to the one call he did hold and managed not to disqualify. It was a nightmare. He interrupted the prospect at every turn. He got basic product information wildly wrong. He had no semblance of next steps. He showed the entire platform when the prospect needed just one thing. The whole situation was cringeworthy. I felt like I needed to take a shower afterward.

I found out later he was disqualifying opportunities that were legitimately qualified, not doing any prospecting for himself, and then blaming marketing and sales development for his low performance.

Six months later and many, many thousands of dollars in his salary wasted, Brett was gone forever.

The funny thing about sales is that it's a great equalizer. You can't hide from your number. Some people find this to be the biggest annoyance about sales. Sure, it gets to me too. But on the bright side, it doesn't matter who your parents were or what background you have; your sales are your sales, and there's no getting around it. You can even have more experience and technically not be as good as someone else.

So, when Brett posted zero dollars in revenue for six months straight, the executives were all shocked. I was not. Not because I am any smarter, but simply because I was on the ground. I could see and hear Brett's behaviors and words in action. Sales are not drummed up magically, nor can you hide from bad numbers behind smooth talking and lip service. So, the disconnect between whatever happened in the hiring process that we apparently skipped over and his performance on the sales floor was very real and very painful.

So, what can we learn from Brett and other real scenarios? To my mind, there are eight cardinal rules that every salesperson ought to follow. Let's look at each one in depth.

RULE #1: NEVER STOP PROSPECTING

An old mentor of mine coined a term decades ago and shared it with me whenever I got overconfident and stopped doing the things that originally made me successful. He called it *executivitis.*

I see this happen on the sales floor frequently. We learn the ropes through prospecting as the very first sales skill, and then because of the rejection, monotony, or whatever mental blockade of excuses we create for ourselves, we stop doing it. We stop doing the thing that feeds us and let other people do it for us, and in doing so we also give away a bit of the ownership in reaching our goals. Prospecting is a skill that should forever be honed and never forgotten, regardless of experience level.

RULE #2: PLAY TO YOUR STRENGTHS

Some people have more success with one channel over another. Some people are amazing writers, while others are great on the phone. I always try to coach to people's strengths and help them get at least a bit better on the areas of weakness. I still recommend salespeople make at least some calls, even if it's not the 150 calls per day I used to make.

Another mentor of mine used to say, "Know a lot about many things, but be really good at one." I think this applies to sales as well. Doubling down on your strengths, while being a student at all the other areas of sales, is crucial.

When I started out as a seller, I booked most of my meetings via phone calls, but more recently I have spent a great deal of time prospecting on social media. I know several people that are phenomenal at emails. Pick your strength and really lean into it, but also diversify by doing at least some work to use and get better at other channels.

RULE #3: MULTICHANNELING IS A MUST

We should also have multiple channels to our approach and not rely solely on one channel. Analyzing messaging is critically important, but so is the act of engaging with buyers in different ways. Even if our preference is for one channel over another, we can miss opportunities by not diversifying. This is analogous to how investors think about diversifying with their portfolios. Diversifying helps you do more with less. And as I said in chapter 6, it helps you become memorable in a world that can't remember your name.

It also serves another purpose: meeting buyers where they are—on their terms, in their preferred mediums. It's also good to get people to see you in many places so that when they are ready to do business with you, you've already stood out.

Here are some sample channels to consider:

- Phone calls
- Emails
- Voicemail
- Events
- Social media
- In person
- Direct mail
- Video prospecting
- Gifting

RULE #4: MULTITHREADING IS ALSO A MUST

Multichanneling means having different ways you reach out. *Multithreading* means prospecting not just one person but different people based on their titles. The best way to do this is to have persona-based messaging for each title in a company. (Remember: *persona* is just a fancy way of saying "job title.") So now we're getting into the territory of prospecting entire accounts, not just one person within them. This helps us navigate the dynamic of companies buying in teams, while also providing contextual information about each team member's motivations and concerns, based on their role.

Multithreading should be highly targeted, and it doesn't mean prospecting everyone. It means prospecting people that might be relevant for you to talk to. Multithreading becomes even more important once a prospect becomes a customer. Is your only contact a single champion? Get some favor with mid-level management, end users, and other senior members of the team.

RULE #5: FOSTER A GROWTH MINDSET

It's so rare to encounter a salesperson who is just on top of it. They are so certain of themselves, their craft, their game, and they take it seriously. They take it so seriously that they make you want to sit up a little straighter in your chair. So frequently, sales calls are put together haphazardly. We ran five sales calls today and we're tired, so we slump and don't speak with confidence. We have an "OK, whatever" mindset.

Someone with a growth mindset has the opposite attitude. They are incredibly well versed in the landscape and can even make recommendations that their buyer might not know about. It goes without saying that they're on top of their own product. They know it inside and out—not because the people with the most product knowledge are necessarily the best sellers, but because in the age of the buyer, the buyers themselves have more knowledge, and so these sellers know they must keep up.

They also take responsibility for their own success and learning. They *own* their results, whether good or bad. And they almost always take the emotion out of their performance. Instead, if there are ever performance issues, they try to get to the heart of why something happens, come up with a hypothesis, and then formulate a plan on how they think they can be better. The salespeople with the greatest ownership end up being top performers over time and even beat out others with more raw talent.

Two great books on this topic are *Extreme Ownership* by Jocko Willink and Leif Babin and *Mindset: The New Psychology of Success* by Carol Dweck. I recommend checking both out.

RULE #6: CHANGE UP YOUR CTAS

CTA means "call to action." It's usually the ask you have for prospects and customers.

Buyers' sensory systems are assaulted by salespeople daily. Buyers have ask fatigue when it comes to salespeople. "Can I get fifteen minutes on your calendar?" has become a visceral and immediate way we try to engage with them. Everyone asks it. So, when everyone shifts left, you go right. Don't only reach out when you want something. And don't say the same thing everyone else is saying.

Case in point: the Guinness World Record holder for the most cars sold in a year, Joe Girard, claimed his success wasn't only because of his sales gifts but also because he would send postcards to his entire list every month. So maybe you even eliminate CTAs on some of your messaging.

This is relevant to people who sell over the phone or digitally as well, using multiple channels for follow-ups. For example, with a voicemail or a social media touch, I might not even ask for a reply to that specific message but direct them to some other message I have sent. I also don't ask for something in return on every channel—in fact, I try to limit the asks. Buyers are accustomed to salespeople always asking for something, so when you don't do things the same way as everyone else, you stand out. A typical ask buyers get is "Are you available next week for a fifteen-minute demo?" I highly recommend testing out different CTAs and measuring the results for each. Emphasize starting a conversation more than trying to get someone on a demo of your product.

RULE #7: NEVER SHOW UP UNPREPARED

Brett was almost never prepared for his calls. He would show up and say whatever came to mind, then be reactive to whatever it was the prospect said, without much thought. This sounds extreme, but it happens with all sorts of sellers. We've all had calls where we might not be the most prepared.

Two exercises I encourage to help get myself out of this pattern are pre-call planning and account planning.

PRE-CALL PLANNING

Pre-call planning is the activity of researching a company, a person, and the purpose for the call, then jotting down the goal of your call and the most important information you have going in, what you'll need while you're in the call, and goals for next steps.

My formula:

> Outcome of previous call (if any):
> Goal of this call (them):
> Goal of this call (me):
> Ideal next step:
> Actors:
> Pain:
> Their reasons for speaking:
> Tools using:
> What they care about:

Feel free to lengthen or shorten the model above. The important thing here is get in the mode of preparation. You run the play in your head first, and this enables you to be nimbler on an actual call. Imagine a basketball player who anticipates another team's plays before they run them. This anticipated preparation is one small step to standing apart. It's very easy to show up to back-to-back meetings. It takes much more discipline to show up prepared. Writing these details down forces us to make sure we are taking our calls in the direction we want them to go. We control what we *can* control.

ACCOUNT PLANNING

Another extremely powerful yet underutilized tool for selling is account planning. Account plans capture all the most important details of an account. It's your living, breathing document. It is your internal strategy tool that documents the pertinent information about accounts and customers.

Some items you might list in an account plan:

- Everyone involved on your side
- Everyone involved on their side
- Their goals
- Your goals
- Main competitors
- Relevant industry insights
- Insights on the people involved
- Insights on the personas/roles you are selling to
- Challenges
- Expansion goals

You should also include your action plan and ideal dates for each action.

Account plans are internal and not customer facing, but you often take information from the plan to then show customers—in quarterly business reviews, for example. The idea is that these plans are much more robust than what you would capture after any given call. This is your guide to an account—your atlas, even. It's an incredibly powerful tool to get internal alignment around your customer or prospect objectives.

RULE #8: ASK, DON'T TELL

Sales is about asking questions to solve problems. Yet so many sellers lead with telling. Even when we do ask questions, there's often room for improvement because too often they come across as helping us more than helping to get to root causes of buyers' problems.

Auditing our questions is the best way to get better at sales. Telling pushes; asking pulls. Asking doesn't mean asking a lot of questions. It means asking effective questions. Effective questions get to the point in the least number of questions, while gaining maximum information and helping the customer realize their own objectives as well. Questions are our conduit to selling in a way that is conversational rather than rigid. Too often, though, we don't ask the right questions, so they end up sounding interrogational instead of conversational.

The following table includes specific questions buyers hate and what you can say instead.

GOOD AND BAD QUESTIONS TO ASK BUYERS

Poor Sales Experience Questions	Positive Sales Experience Questions
Does that make sense?	→What are your thoughts on this specific part? →How would you envision this working? →What about that is intriguing?
What is your budget?	→ Would it make sense to discuss pricing?
Is there anything I can send?	→ What materials would be most useful in helping you communicate with your team? →What would be motivating for people who aren't on the call today to see?
Do you think this is a good fit?	→ In your own words, can you tell me how this might work? →How could you see your team using this?
Do you have time for a follow-up next week?	→ What time works best for you? →When would it make sense to speak again?

Do you have any questions?	→ What questions can I answer?
Is there anyone else that needs to be involved?	→ What does Suzie care most about? →Who else would be involved in this?
Should we set next steps?	→ Would it be OK if we spoke about our plan of action here?
What do you know about us?	→ Here's what I've learned about you all . . .
Are you a decision maker?	→ How have you handled previous decisions most like this one?

Here's a bonus of additional questions you can ask to help improve with prospects and customers alike:

"How do you see this working in your organization?"

"Would it make sense to talk about . . . ?"

"Have you considered . . . ?"

"What about . . . ?"

"How would it work if . . . ?"

"What are your thoughts on . . . ?"

"Can we walk through . . . ?"

If there's one final takeaway here, it's that great questions breathe oxygen into our calls. They don't make buyers feel defensive; they are disarming and even-keeled, and they get to the next steps faster than self-serving questions. Thoughtful questioning is the key to repeated and sustained success in sales.

TRY THIS

- Never stop prospecting. The best sellers keep this skill sharpened. What if another department's well dries up? You are still equipped to make money and hit your own goals.
- Create a pre-call template that works for you, and spend five minutes before each call jotting your ideas and notes down.
- Attitude and mindset are everything in sales. It's often not what happens *to* us in sales but how we *respond*. Foster a growth mindset.
- Focus on skills acquisition and not just experience. Focus on repeated results through sales skills, regardless of tenure.
- Play to your strengths but also learn in your areas of growth.
- Multichannel and multithread your sales efforts.

CHAPTER 8

YOUR JOB IS NOT YOUR LIFE

HOW TO NAVIGATE THE HUMAN ASPECTS OF SELLING

One summer morning when I was twenty-six, I woke up and did my normal routine. I got up, got dressed, went to work. I was working downtown in a midsized city, where all the big high rises were. I was responsible for closing new business at a startup where I was working. I was decent at this. Definitely a harder sale than my first sales role, but still, I was off to a decent start.

On this particular morning, I started out in a relatively good mood. I grabbed my morning cup of coffee on the way in and went about my normal day. A couple hours into the day, I put on my headset and got on a demo with a prospect. Then, out of the blue, I started sweating profusely. I could feel my pulse racing.

I had never had a panic attack before, so I didn't know what was happening. I was terrified. It was like reaching the summit of a roller-coaster ride and then plunging into the low curl of

I had never had a panic attack before, so I didn't know what was happening.

the trough without a seat belt on. I have no idea how I made it through that sales call, but I did. Thank God the person on the other line was probably the nicest prospect I had ever spoken to. But I still botched the call completely.

Afterward, I went outside to get some fresh air. There was this lingering feeling, like right after someone punches you in the head. I knew that feeling all too well from my years in karate, but at least then we had gloves on. This was like an actual punch to the head, a constant fluttering of the heart, and a sinking feeling in my stomach all at once. It felt like a death spiral.

"Tuso, you OK?" a friend asked.

"Yeah, I'm fine. Just tired is all."

I didn't want to talk, but I didn't want to be alone either. I just sort of sat there, listening to a couple of coworkers riff on the day, the job, some incompetent new hire, whatever. I don't really remember what they were saying.

There was no obvious reason for me to have a panic attack that day. The lady on the other end of the call was super nice and calm. And she was actually listening to me, unlike most of my sales calls back then. But I guess that's how it goes with our mind. There doesn't always have to be a reason for something to happen. It just happens. What's almost worse is that things like this seem to always happen at completely the wrong time. Like on a sales call when you're trying to be an example for your team.

Except in my case, I was determined to find that reason. This was 2015, and it would be another two years before I got a grip on that day. It wasn't that the panic attacks persisted per se, but the anxiety from years of selling—years of life, really—did. I wasn't coming at my job from a place of sustainable energy. I had worked in a toxic atmosphere where leadership encouraged the numbing of emotions via the constant consumption of caffeine and alcohol. At one point, they installed

$20,000 coffee machines so we wouldn't leave the office during the day. They also paid for our dinner to encourage us to stay late. Instead of feeling like a legitimate perk, it kind of felt like another way to handcuff us to our chairs.

The only real thing they were encouraging was stress. All these supposed perks felt like trickery, and the constant pressure led to burnout. It was always "make more dials" without explaining how to get better at sales. And burned out I was. It was like I was in an abusive relationship. I can hear a therapist just saying the words, "What we need to figure out is why you allowed your abuser to take it that far." Except my abuser was my job. I was doing well financially, but I was miserable.

At some point I started to realize the more bells and whistles a company has hanging around ornamentally like that— the coffee, Ping-Pong, lunches, dinner, and booze—the more they're probably trying to hide. There's not enough Ping-Pong in the world to mask a difficult job. But a difficult job I can deal with. It's the terrible workplace that always gets to me.

I wasn't taking care of myself either. I had stopped going to the gym. I wasn't doing any of the activities that made me happy. Burned out from work, I wasn't seeing friends as usual anymore. I was deeply attached to my professional success, yet no matter how well I did, success always felt so far away.

About two years later, I was working at a different startup in Los Angeles when a salesperson from Headspace, which makes a popular meditation app, came into our office to give a presentation. The entire company gathered at lunchtime and heard him speak. At his direction, we then all closed our eyes and meditated for ten minutes together. I was skeptical at first. I was thinking to myself, *This is so LA, meditating at work.* I had never really done it before except for the two-minute sessions I had at the tail end of karate class as a teenager. But back then I had no idea what I was doing. I never followed my breath, and I mostly just daydreamed. *I wonder what's for dinner?* doesn't exactly qualify as an introspective thought or following your breath. But in this instance, now that I was a sliver more mature, I actually followed my breath. I tried to look at my thoughts from an objective outsider's view instead of the normal chasing each thought. This time I was relaxed. Mindful, even.

At home one night a few weeks later, I did a three-minute meditation on my own. Nothing too earth-shattering, but it was a start. I kept this up for two more months, gradually increasing until I was doing at least ten minutes a day. By the third month I was noticing huge differences. More important, people were coming up and telling me that they'd noticed a difference in me.

"You just seem so much lighter," a teammate proclaimed. And I really did feel lighter!

The first change I noticed was clarity of thought. Like, way clearer thinking. I was able to analyze problems and get them solved much quicker. The meditation provided a little wedge I needed to get ahold of the stress associated with building a rapidly growing team. I began to process my stress instead of bottle it. I became immensely more aware. My team and I were much more in sync as a result. My relationships got better. My focus got better. My thinking got better. I started reading more. I started working out like I did before I got into sales. I made a commitment to meditate every single day. I started to have fun.

Once I had gained a little bit of mental clarity, I realized that it was time for a career redirect. I realized that I wasn't in love with my job, and that didn't serve me or my team.

So, I quit.

Quitting a job I wasn't in love with was one of the most liberating things I have ever done. And to go to an early-stage startup where I could build out a team? People said that I was crazy for taking such a risk, but I knew it was the right thing.

In hindsight it was ten times better than my expectations. I had learned to hamper those in favor of a hard look at reality.

Looking back, I can see that meditation has singularly been the biggest positive force of my professional and personal adult life. It's helped me in more ways that I can enumerate. It's gotten me to a more sustainable place in my relationship to work and in life in general. It enabled me to listen better and be more present with buyers. *Work is a part of life and not the other way around.* It created space.

It wasn't just the meditation, though. It was the meditation that led to the clarity of thought, which led to dietary changes, which also led to exercising more, which led to reading more and doing more self-care. The cumulative effect of meditation, compounded by all these other microimprovements in my life, had an enormous impact. One of the biggest things I learned was what I would and would not accept. I learned how to win the game going on introspectively so that I could win externally. At this critical juncture at the ripe age of twenty-eight, I said, "OK, enough. Let's build a team the right way."

And that's exactly what we did.

SALES IS AN ENERGY GAME

Meditation made me realize that the best way to be good at sales isn't just to read all the books and close all the deals but to be able to perform with longevity, with sustainability. Sales is an energy game. I have never in my life seen salespeople struggle with technical tasks, sending an email, or physically making a cold call. I have seen, almost every day of my sales life, someone struggling with their emotions, struggling to be consistent, struggling with burnout, and struggling to be motivated. Struggling with the details of it all. This is what makes sales a craft.

Work is a part of life and not the other way around.

This is also why sales is mostly a soft skill. Not just because soft skills are required to work with buyers. Soft skills help us manage ourselves. It's hard to go to work and sell a product and deal with rejection all day if you haven't done the work of building a life that you are happy with in general. Master yourself first and your sales second, and then you'll end up taking care of the buyer and driving real results. Never stop doing the things in your life that you love as a sacrifice for sales. It doesn't work. That's why I had a panic attack. I was so beyond burned out and unhappy because I had stopped doing everything I loved.

What's more, what good is it if I do really well one month and then completely burn myself out the next? It's not sustainable for the company or, more important, for me. Huge peaks and troughs in our own performance have just as much to do with managing our energy as they do with forecasting deals correctly, yet we hardly talk about the emotional side of sales in this light.

Three rules have helped me here:

1. Take your paid time off (PTO). Time off is crucial for mental health.
2. Download a meditation app on your phone. Try creating a habit to use it at the same time every day, without pressuring yourself.
3. Realize that life is first and work is second.

WIN OR LEARN

My years of learning along the way had much more to do with learning how to work better than they did with getting better at sales itself. I reached success in sales early on, but the battle with myself to do well in the long run persisted.

People never talk about the emotional side of sales. The rejection. The burnout. Most books I've read were about the technical side of forecasting: how to progress a prospect through the funnel. Hitting a sales slump is deemed a side effect of not prospecting enough. It's hard to prospect more if you are running on empty.

I love this quote attributed to Nelson Mandela: "I never lose. I either win or learn." In sales, we're either in the *zone of learning* or the *zone of stress*. There are no other zones to choose from, so we might as well choose to learn.

For me, learning began with paying attention to my habits, understanding that the daily microhabits, often the things that are easy to forget, are usually the things we should be paying most attention to. I stopped paying as much attention to goals like "be a head of sales" and "close *x* amount of revenue" and swapped them out with daily habits that would set me on a more successful trajectory. I still have goals that I consider ambitious. But I focus more on mapping *how* to get there through what I *do* daily.

Not only did this work better, but it was so much better for my mental health. I stopped caring where I was in relation to people my age, or what other people had. I was focused on my journey. The comparison I strive for today is being better than myself yesterday or where I was a month or two ago. The irony is I felt better, and that helped me become a top performer.

It took me a long time to get to this point. In college and for a few years after, I was the workaholic type. I enjoyed working. I still do. But I have since learned the value of play, rejuvenation, and energy—that if you have great habits, you can bounce back from pretty much anything. And in a profession where bouncing back is an absolute requirement, it was about time I focused on putting the proper infrastructure in place to help with this.

For me, it boils down to these six essential reminders:

1. Focus on intrinsic versus extrinsic motivators.
2. Get back to the things you love. Use them to support what you do in sales.
3. Get back to the right people, exercise, and diet.
4. Meditate daily and get a proper amount of sleep.
5. Pick your boss and get rid of any tyrannical business environments.
6. Realize your ability to hit a number does not define who you are as a person. Detach from the outcome.

I go back to this list with great regularity. In good times, but especially when I don't feel 100 percent. It works for helping me get better at sales—a lifelong pursuit of mine. It's the biggest project I have undertaken in sales. For me it was taking things into my own hands, because until you do that, everything about sales feels like it is happening *to* you instead of *because of* you. You must feel like the governor of your own life. It's wired into who we are.

DON'T GO IT ALONE

When I first started out in sales, I felt like I knew absolutely nothing. One of my mentors, Anna McMahon, looked at me and said, "Listen to me, you're going to be really good at this." And that's all I needed to hear. It didn't matter that I had no idea how to close a deal or I felt pressured to build a pipeline while I was also learning the ropes in what felt like an impossible juggling act. I had one person sit me down, look me in the eyes, and say, "You got this." Anna is still my mentor today.

Just like selling is not a passive exercise, finding a mentor is not either. Through developing relationships over an entire career, you will meet an enormous array of people. The single most useful element to my career (other than meditation) has been having a network of mentors. But even just one mentor can make a massive difference. Cultivating deep, meaningful professional and personal relationships with people who can help you advance through life and your career is the ultimate secret sauce. You can be intentional about how you go about this. Are you the kind of person people want to invest time in?

Mentors help you reach your aspirations, hold you accountable, and guide you in mastering your craft. Mine have been teachers of how to prospect and close deals, all the way up to starting a business. I would never have been successful in any of my professional pursuits without my mentors. They were even the driving force behind this book.

When you find a mentor and advance in your career, always make sure to pay it forward by offering to help others for free as well. None of us got to where we are on our own. Chances are someone took a chance on you. Some mentor reached out and said, "Hey, this way, over here." If you rise to a position where you can help others like this, make sure you pay it forward.

GET PROMOTED BY CHANGING IT UP

One of my reps, Jerry, pulled me aside one day and asked if we could go on a walk. He had been in his role for two months and hit a ramping quota twice. He got right to the point.

"So, Tuso, I've been thinking, and you know, I really think I would make a great account executive."

Jerry wanted to get promoted, and this walk meant he was going to convince me how. Unfortunately for him, he would have done better if he'd treated me a little more like a prospect. What if instead of asking directly, he'd tried to discover organically what I cared about in people getting promoted? It wasn't time that I cared about. It was preparedness. I generally preferred at least six months in the entry-level role because I saw a trend of people fizzling out in the next role if they were promoted too quickly.

The second biggest piece of advice I would offer to Jerry is that if you want a job, first do the work of the job you want, to make it a no-brainer for the people who approve it. Instead of selling me on why he should have this next job, he could have showed me through his actions. He could have conducted discovery to see what I thought was needed to get there. Then he could have taken action on those pieces of advice, and then I would have gone from blocker to advocate. And while I always support making intentions known publicly, actions speak louder than words, especially when you're trying to get promoted.

What are some actions you can take to do the job before you have it? Here are a few things:

- Make sure you're hitting all your current goals and expectations in your current role.
- Discover what your immediate manager cares most about with promotions.
- See what activities you can do that don't take away from your current job in terms of focus but might be a bridge to a future job opportunity.
- Craft a business case or proposal for your efforts to learn more.

Other actionable tips for moving to a new role:

- Listen to and score calls.
- Interview people in the role you want.
- Shadow people in the role you want.

- Read all relevant enablement and training materials.
- Ask what resources your colleagues recommend.

Don't let your performance dip, though. Usually, managers strongly dislike it when someone is doing the job of another role without having mastered their current one. This can be a blocker to getting promoted.

The last thing I might say to Jerry is to run toward, not away. It was clear from our conversation that Jerry was running away from his current role to the next one, instead of running toward the next one. As a manager, I was resistant to this dynamic because when I saw people running from one role to the next, I often saw that dynamic repeated—once they got to the next role, they would try to run from that one too. I tried to encourage Jerry to slow it all down and focus on building his skill set. No one can take that away from you. A title, they most certainly can.

CONTROL THE CONTROLLABLE

Here's the thing about sales: You can learn all the tips and tricks. You can follow what all the thought leaders say. You can try your very best to nail every sales tactic and methodology. And having done so, you'll be much more likely than others to be successful. But to gain real mastery, to gain longevity, to find that deep-seated sense of purpose, you will need to master the emotional side of sales—the energy part. The part where you're able to tolerate rejection and monotony. What job doesn't have these things? All jobs have them, but not like ours. Anyone can do sales, but so few are great sellers.

With so many moving pieces, we know the key to doing well is focusing on what we can control and not getting bogged down by the many elements that are not within that control. I have interviewed thousands of people and managed hundreds of salespeople. The single most important quality to sustained success in sales is believing you have a high locus of control. That means believing your surroundings and success are governed by your own actions and not happening to you. The most successful salespeople see themselves as the governors of their success and failure, and they don't blame anyone else. Foster this mindset alone, and you'll be better than 90 percent of your peers.

So, for me, crafting the sale isn't a destination, a checkbox to mark, or a place to reach; sales is a journey to constantly get better at the craft, but doing so in a way that is sustainable across an entire career. Burnout is the enemy of creativity, and we are in a profession where we could use a whole lot more creativity.

Getting better at working on yourself means learning your own self-worth all over again. Changing for the better. It means knowing where to go where you will be valued, and when that value is no longer seen, you have an obligation to yourself to end that relationship.

TRY THIS

- ◆ Focus on some of your intrinsic motivations. The one rule is that it can't be about money. Write these down. Go beyond "What is my why?" What do you enjoy? What will make you feel balanced when you're at work as well?
- ◆ Download a meditation app and test out a few sessions. Try to keep with it even when it might seem like work or even boring.
- ◆ Create unmovable blocks of time in your calendar for activities and hobbies you enjoy.
- ◆ What do you like about sales as a career? Write these things down somewhere so you can refer to them on the hard days. What do you dislike? Write this down too. Sometimes building awareness can be huge, helping us focus on the parts we like and learn to appreciate the parts we don't like as well.
- ◆ What are some habits you would like to cultivate? Visualize these mentally.
- ◆ What are the top three ways you can relieve stress to help yourself bounce back? Write these down on a sheet of paper.

THE UNCOMMON SALESPERSON

WHY A GOOD SALES EXPERIENCE MAKES BUSINESS BETTER FOR EVERYONE

A few months ago, I went car shopping with my partner. At the first dealership, we had a frictionless experience. We asked to test-drive a car we liked without the salesperson, and he readily agreed. When we got back, the salesperson asked if we had any questions. I asked a few questions, which he answered briefly and honestly. When I told him we needed to think about it before buying, he said, "OK, great, no pressure from me." And we went on our way.

That same day we went to a second dealership. We went on a test-drive, but the salesperson insisted on going with us. When we said we had an appointment and needed to go and that we would think about it, he proceeded to go into pitch mode, listing all the features of the car and the awards they had won. He also offered us a big discount off the sticker price preemptively.

"I wouldn't wait on this deal," he said. "Our features are so much better than the competition." He then literally followed us outside the store, still shouting at us inaudibly.

It's probably no surprise that we ended up going with the first dealer. Not that there wasn't space for that seller to improve—there was plenty. But overall, the sales experience was very straightforward. We came in, asked our questions, got them answered, and test-drove, and then we compared this dealer to the competition. The seller made it very easy for us to come back to him, and that's exactly what we did.

So how could the first salesman have improved? Sales isn't about letting people take test-drives and leaving things up to chance, although matching exactly what they want with what you have is often powerful enough. The problem is he had no idea what we were looking for, so he was hoping. When sellers leave it up to chance, buyers are likely to favor the status quo, which usually does not help the buyer make the decision to buy the car they need. A simple noninvasive question or two would have done the trick here. So, the second car salesman should have been less pushy, but the first should have asked some questions to try to meet our potential need. He should have tried to identify and solve our problem. Were we looking for a minivan or an Audi?

Another interesting situation like this came up recently with a colleague. I asked him to recount his purchase experience with a software company, and his entire demeanor changed. He stiffened, and the pitch in his voice rose.

"I told them we wanted a discount, and they dropped the price by $20,000. The salesperson probably thought they were being buyer-centric, but it really made me mad. How could they drop a price so fast, so easily? This was a really established company with supposedly well-thought-out sales practices."

So much of the time when we think we're being buyer-centric, we're not. Going from a $60,000 price tag to a $40,000 price tag so quickly caused the buyer to rethink the whole transaction. It inserted doubt into the equation. *Why didn't they just start off with $40,000 if it was so easy to drop the price?* This was not a novice company either. This was a company that had recently been acquired by a larger company for $1 billion.

The salesperson would have been wiser to pause and ask a question. Any question would have been better than what he did. Maybe something like "You're a really valued customer, and continuing our partnership is very important to us. Can you talk to me more about your concern with this amount?"

Instead of jumping to solve for every problem we encounter, we're much better off if we learn. It's hard to focus on the details of selling if all we do is pitch what we think matters most instead of listening.

Many of the people I meet who work in sales are go-getters. They want to get things done. That's a good thing. Being able to make things happen and move deals forward is a skill in and of itself. But often what's most required is pausing, reflecting, and asking before making a move. Don't pounce on your prospects and customers!

BE HONEST WITH BUYERS

I was managing a sales team at a startup in Los Angeles when one day I noticed a bunch of my team members flocking to the kitchen.

"Tuso, there's this really awesome company here. They are serving juice that comes out of this amazing machine, and it's absolutely delicious. Go try some!"

It wasn't completely random. We would routinely have

companies come in and let us try their products, hoping to sell to the employees or to have our company become customers. Everyone was so into companies like the one whose juice I was about to try.

So, I went to the kitchen and lined up to try the juice. When it was my turn, I watched the employee representative from the company grab a modern-looking bag. It looked almost like the cool packaging you would find in the snack aisle of Whole Foods. Very elegant. Then he placed the bag in this contraption that looked like a cross between a blender and a thicker Mac laptop propped up on a white pedestal. He opened the machine up, placed the bag inside, then closed the machine, and juice would dispense.

Voilà!

I said something along the lines of "How does this work?"

"Cool, isn't it?" the representative replied. "The machine applies eight hundred pounds of pressure on these packets. Inside the packets are your favorite fruits and veggies. When the machine applies pressure to the packet, out dispenses pure juice. It's like magic. Instead of buying processed juice from the store, you can now have the freshest juice right at home or the office. It really is quite amazing."

"Wow, that really is quite amazing. How do you get the packets? How does the pricing work?" I inquired.

The employee explained that you had to buy the machine for around $700, and then each packet was five to eight dollars. Expensive, he acknowledged, but worth it.

I tried the juice, finished up the conversation with some niceties, and went back to my desk. I have to say, the juice was good, but I wasn't about to pay $700 for it.

They ended up visiting our office at least one more time. During their next visit, I would repeat the experience almost identically with a different representative. I ended up researching the company, noticing they had an enormous financial backing and really seemed to be the real deal on the surface. All the right institutional investors from Silicon Valley. They were also targeting the right types of people and companies. It seemed like they were doing well and, more importantly, they were onto something.

Except they weren't. Not even close.

The company was Juicero. They went from massive success to overnight catastrophe after an article by *Bloomberg* broke. Apparently, you could just take the packets and squeeze them with your hands and the juice would dispense without the use of the machine. The whole "eight hundred pounds of pressure" story was a farce. A total flop of a product. News followed the *Bloomberg* story left and right. Another headline from the *Guardian* read, "Squeezed Out: Widely Mocked Startup Juicero Is Shutting Down."

Members of the company, as well as investors, were quick to defend that they knew the juice could be dispensed by hand, but that people preferred the machine because it was less messy. No one was buying it.

Juicero ended up refunding people and closing its doors later that year. They had amassed over $118 million in funding. The CEO, Doug Evans, dubbed himself the Steve Jobs of juice. Investors loved the recurring-revenue subscription model that the company offered and got starry-eyed over the look and feel of the machine and the storyline given by the company.

Juicero sold a product on a false premise. There are countless stories like this one, where you can't even begin to craft a sales experience because it's built on a lie. You can't sell a product that doesn't solve a problem. That's not sales.

The first lesson of sales is that you must start with a phenomenal product. If you don't start with that, your battle is going to be an uphill one. It's not enough to be good at any one function anymore. Because it has never been easier to build products, companies must be great at all disciplines to remain competitive. They must be good at sales, marketing, product, the works. For us as sellers, it means choosing places to work where leadership understands sales, but also has the other parts of the business going well. The reality is everyone should care about the sales experience because without it there is no business. An engineer is building a product that salespeople can sell, and so they too should have a glimpse into this. Everyone at a company functions to generate revenue and ultimately a profit. Without it, a business cannot survive. Maybe most companies aren't like Juicero, or most people aren't like its founder, building a company on a lie. But every company can go further when it comes to sales, product, marketing, and creating a powerful sales experience.

But treating sales as a craft means not settling for mediocrity but rather striving for what is within reach but difficult to attain. It's focusing on the small details that help us level up our game. We spend too much time at work not to treat it this way—as something worth pursuing and improving. That's why I've been so excited to see people choosing sales as a profession instead of falling into it. Universities are even teaching sales courses. I think if there was one skill that could be taught to everyone across the world to lift them out of poverty and give them valuable abilities that transferred to other disciplines, it would be sales.

I once had a manager who used to say, "You can't outsell math." The same way you can't outsell math, you also can't fake success. You have to put in the work.

YOU CAN'T SELL EVERYONE

And so, I will leave you with this: *not everyone is going to be your customer today.* That is completely fine and a fact you should internalize. But in the world of people who could possibly buy today, will they choose you? Will you work in such a way that you earn their business? Or will they slide off to a competitor or, worse, revert to the status quo?

One of the main ideas behind sales is making sure that when buyers are in the market for your type of product, *yours* is the one they choose to buy. This requires an earnest effort to play the long game. It requires commitment and discipline. It requires you to not give in to the temptation to pitch all the time and instead ask meaningful questions that unveil.

It's ending the charade of spamming our prospects and re-placing that with the thoughtfulness of improving efficiency and effectiveness everywhere possible. It's coming to work from a place of strength and abundance instead of desperation and fear. It's pacing your tone to be slower and more deliberate instead of fast and nervous. It's the confidence to face rejection day in and day out, knowing that it doesn't define or affect who you are as a person. It's detaching from the outcome so that you don't start coupling self-worth to your quota attainment.

It's inserting creativity into your social media posts and emails so they speak to people on an emotional level, because that is what you also respond to as a human being. It's audit-ing how you treat leads to optimize for ease and what makes sense for the buyer experience as opposed to your internal convenience. It's the peer-to-peer learning and growth that sets you up for success, because blind spots are best noticed by people who are not us, and both the seller and the buyer gain a great deal when we do this. It's not practicing on our prospects, but putting in work to improve outside of our live calls and interactions with buyers. It's the constant feedback built into the organization so we aren't testing out unchecked theories on our prospects without first having vetted them for easy feedback.

It's taking ownership of our own learning, because we can't control how good our manager is, only how good we want to

And so, I will leave you with this: *not everyone is going to be your customer today.* That is completely fine and a fact you should internalize. But in the world of people who could possibly buy today, will they choose you? Will you work in such a way that you earn their business? Or will they slide off to a competitor or, worse, revert to the status quo?

be. It's not saying, "That's the way we've always done it," but instead fostering creative ways to solve old problems. It's not seeing the world as "only one way to do things," because as with math, you can get to the same result in myriad ways.

It's taking the time to score our own calls and those of others, because reflecting with frameworks in hand is a great way to highlight how we can improve. It's not just feeling great about our jobs when things are going well for us but also putting forth that same effort when things are not going so well. It's taking our PTO so we feel refreshed, and realizing that work is a part of our life, not our entire life. It's being committed to being a lifelong learner, because those are the only people that ever really make a difference.

All of this and more is achievable because we live in a world of abundance. If we act with earnestness and dedication, believing not just that it's the right thing to do but that it's good for business and for people, we can all be better and thrive at work and in life as well.

And that is when we start treating the sales profession as a craft worthy of mastery.

ACKNOWLEDGMENTS

The first person I must thank is Andy Paul. Andy's outreach to me is perhaps the biggest reason this book ever came into existence. He came to me at the right time in my life and was instrumental to me taking the important first step toward completing a manuscript. He also helped guide me throughout the process as he is an experienced author himself. I will always remember Andy's mentorship as pivotal to me writing my first book.

The next two people I must thank are Bill Cross and Polly Greist, who reviewed many meticulous details with me throughout the process and often heard the day-to-day level frustrations, wins, and minutiae that went into this book. Your support and help have been invaluable to me.

Trena White made many important introductions, which ultimately landed me on Girl Friday for the publication of this book. Trena is a titan in the book world. She has both the grace that makes you want to talk to her and the professional prowess that makes you trust her and want to work with her. Thank you.

Marni Seneker was the one who got the words out of my head and on to the page. This was a herculean task, and she was the perfect person for me at that part of the journey. Dan Crissman took those words on the page and helped me transform them. First by helping me realize that I wrote the wrong book, and then working with me to craft the new one, this one, *Crafting the Sale*. This is the book I was meant to write, and

Dan was instrumental in that journey. Dan is a very skilled editor, and I hope to work with him again.

Reshma Kooner was my day-to-day go-to. She helped me at every stage and was there for the highs and the lows. She was the best project manager I could have asked for. Some days she was my therapist and advocate and on others she was my marketing and sales director. Georgie worked alongside her to really make sure I nailed the marketing side of the book. I can't thank either of them enough.

My sales career would never have taken off without Anna McMahon, whom I mention in the book. Anna sat me down and said, "You got this," and has had my back ever since. The universe bestowed an intelligent and impeccable sales leader and mentor upon me through you.

The last two people I must thank are my mom and my partner, Nick. My mom was diagnosed with cancer while I was writing this book—the month I inked the deal with Girl Friday in fact. At one point I asked, "Do you want me to pause?" and she selflessly asked me to move forward with my life goals, this book especially. Having a mom who offers fierce loyalty and unconditional support to her children has been a driving force of my life and career. I would not have accomplished any of the goals in my life without her quiet yet powerful love.

I also must thank my partner, Nick Cross. Perhaps no one knew my process more intimately than you. Your support has meant everything. Your patience with canceled plans, rescheduled date nights, and my constant workload has been unwavering. I will look back on creating this book as an achievement I can share with you because you were just as much a part of the process as I was. You are my cocreator, and together we are a *team*.

And last, I must thank you, the reader, and all the salespeople I have met over the years. The real secret of this book is that I am *your* student—I am the one still figuring things out and hoping to get better at sales alongside you every day. It's an honor of a lifetime to learn from you.

RESOURCES

BOOKS:

Atomic Habits: An Easy & Proven Way to Build Good Habits & Break Bad Ones by James Clear

The Challenger Sale: Taking Control of the Customer Conversation by Matthew Dixon and Brent Adamson

Extreme Ownership: How U.S. Navy SEALs Lead and Win by Jocko Willink and Leif Babin

Fanatical Prospecting: The Ultimate Guide to Opening Sales Conversations and Filling the Pipeline by Leveraging Social Selling, Telephone, E-mail, Text, and Cold Calling by Jeb Blount

The 15 Commitments of Conscious Leadership: A New Paradigm for Sustainable Success by Jim Dethmer, Diana Chapman, and Kaley Warner Klemp

Influence: Science and Practice by Robert Cialdini

Leaders Eat Last: Why Some Teams Pull Together and Others Don't by Simon Sinek

Mindset: The New Psychology of Success by Carol Dweck

Never Split the Difference: Negotiating As If Your Life Depended on It by Chris Voss

The Presentation Secrets of Steve Jobs: How to Be Insanely Great in Front of Any Audience by Carmine Gallo

Pre-Suasion: A Revolutionary Way to Influence and Persuade by Robert Cialdini

The Sales Development Playbook: Build Repeatable Pipeline and Accelerate Growth with Inside Sales by Trish Bertuzzi

Sales Manager Survival Guide: Lessons from Sales' Front Lines
   by David Brook
*Sell Without Selling Out: A Guide to Success on Your Own
   Terms* by Andy Paul
Thinking, Fast and Slow by Daniel Kahneman

PODCASTS:

The Official SaaStr Podcast
Sales Enablement Podcast with Andy Paul

ABOUT THE AUTHOR

 Michael Tuso has hired, coached, and trained hundreds of salespeople and generated millions in revenue for businesses from startups to Fortune 500 companies. He has served in virtually every sales role there is, from entry-level all the way up to cofounder and CEO of his own startup, Callypso. Prior to beginning Callypso, Michael was the first sales leader at Chili Piper, joining when they had less than $1 million in revenue. By the time he left, he had helped scale them through a Series B valuation of $350 million. He was responsible for hiring, coaching, and training the entire sales organization.

Tuso has been named a two-time Top Sales Leader to Follow by the American Association of Inside Sales Professionals, Best Sales Development Leader by Tenbound, a Top LinkedIn Sales Star by Sales Success Media, and a Top Sales Leader to Follow by Crunchbase. He also sits on the Diversity, Equity, and Inclusion advisory board of SaaSy Sales Leadership, a sales training company.

Tuso is deeply passionate about and intent on spreading his message of fostering meaningful change that will help businesses be more successful and help buyers get their problems solved.

CPSIA information can be obtained
at www.ICGtesting.com
Printed in the USA
JSHW080241140623
43206JS00003B/6